DESPERATELY SEEKING SUSAN FOREMAN

Richard Kirby

DESPERATELY SEEKING SUSAN FOREMAN
©2013 Richard Kirby. All Rights Reserved.
Doctor Who © BBC
No part of this book may be reproduced in any form or by any means, electronic, mechanical, digital, photocopying or recording, except for the inclusion in a review, without permission in writing from the publisher.

Published in the USA by:
BearManor Media
P O Box 71426
Albany, Georgia 31708
www.bearmanormedia.com

ISBN: 978-1-59393-728-7
Printed in the United States of America
Book design by Robbie Adkins
Cover art by Dominic Lea

ACKNOWLEDGEMENTS

Well this is a pleasant surprise! When I first started tapping away on a keyboard, I honestly never expected anyone outside my family and close friends to read my work, so to have *Desperately Seeking Susan Foreman* published is a fantastic feeling, and I'd like to say a massive thank you to Ben, Michelle, Wendy, Robbie and *BearManor Media* for being willing to (in the words of Agnetha and Frida) "take a chance on me." I am both flattered and extremely grateful.

I must also express my appreciation to everyone who took the time to reply to my letters requesting signed photographs for inclusion within these pages—especially given my barely legible handwriting. I would like to say an extra special thank you to those who went one step further and actually wrote back to me: Anneke Wills, Katy Manning, Daphne Ashbrook, the late Caroline John, Wanda Ventham, and Lucy Gaskell.

Thanks also (I'm on a roll now!) to the members of my close and extended family, and friends old and new, who have read one/some/most of my books and sent comments, reviews—and even photos! You gave me the confidence to keep writing in the hope that one day a door might just open.

And finally, to my wife Elaine, thank you for everything. I love you xxx.

CONTENTS

	Page
Acknowledgements	iii
Introduction	vii
Where it All Started	1
Challenge Anneke	13
Daylight Come … Time to Go Home	23
Gail Warning	29
Another Roll of the Dice	39
Looking Good Ma'am	43
Committing Insecticide	49
Deaf to the Daleks	53
The Color Purple	63
All Monsters Great and Small	67
Vision Off	73
Saving Grace	79
The Wait is Over	83
Read it and Weep	91
Oi! Watch it Spaceman!	97
Matt Finish	103
Bibliography	113

This book is fondly dedicated to Elisabeth Sladen, Caroline John, and Mary Tamm

INTRODUCTION

I'm not too sure what the actual numerical definition is of the phrase "by public demand." In the case of this third, and absolutely final, rewrite of *Desperately Seeking Susan Foreman* (the quest to track down all the female traveling companions from *Doctor Who*), the magic number was two!

Caroline and Jackie... I thank you!

In fairness, there is a serious reason for what will be more of a complete reworking rather than a simple cut-and-paste plus update—mainly because I appear to have deleted the original file... yes, clearly I *am* that stupid—and that is to dedicate the book to the collective memory of Lis Sladen, Caroline John, and Mary Tamm, all of whom sent photos—and in Caroline's case letters as well—for inclusion in previous versions and all of whom have since passed away.

So very sad.

Also, since the second edition hit the streets—literally in some cases, I'm led to believe—I am now the proud owner of signed photographs from four more companions. But who are they?

Well you'll just have to read on, however, I can officially confirm that one is either Alex Kingston or Jenna-Louise Coleman: the two new additions to my definitive list of female companions, which follows. I accept that other *Doctor Who* devotees may consider the list is incomplete with arguably inconsistent reasoning for qualification—if that is the case may I be the first to wish you every success with your book.

	Character	**Actress**
1.	Susan Foreman	Carole Ann Ford
2.	Barbara Wright	Jacqueline Hill
3.	Vicki	Maureen O'Brien
4.	Katarina	Adrienne Hill
5.	Dodo Chaplet	Jackie Lane
6.	Polly	Anneke Wills
7.	Victoria Waterfield	Deborah Watling
8.	Zoë Heriot	Wendy Padbury
9.	Liz Shaw	Caroline John
10.	Jo Grant	Katy Manning

11.	Sarah Jane Smith	Elisabeth Sladen
12.	Leela	Louise Jameson
13.	Romana 1	Mary Tamm
14.	Romana 2	Lalla Ward
15.	Nyssa	Sarah Sutton
16.	Tegan Jovanka	Janet Fielding
17.	Peri Brown	Nicola Bryant
18.	Mel Bush	Bonnie Langford
19.	Ace	Sophie Aldred
20.	Grace Holloway	Daphne Ashbrook
21.	Rose Tyler	Billie Piper
22.	Donna Noble	Catherine Tate
23.	Martha Jones	Freema Agyeman
24.	Amy Pond	Karen Gillan
25.	River Song	Alex Kingston
26.	Clara Oswald	Jenna-Louise Coleman

I suppose the book is primarily aimed at readers with an interest in *Doctor Who*, and perhaps unfairly I have assumed a reasonable level of prior knowledge about the various incarnations of the Doctor as well as some of the other regular characters and enemies that have featured over what is rapidly approaching fifty years of televised time travel.

If any lack of background at a particular point spoils your enjoyment of the book, then I apologize; not enjoying the book because you think it's rubbish—well that's something totally different!

So, just to briefly map out what is going to follow: the signed companion photos will be supplemented by one or two others I acquired along the way. There will be new written bits combined with the best of the old stuff from the October 2011 version, and because I had to retype everything, you will have the satisfaction of knowing that whilst the book might have cost you a bit of money, it's cost me the feeling in most of my fingers.

WHERE IT ALL STARTED

By 17:16 on Saturday, November 23, 1963, the New Zealand All Blacks had emerged victorious over a Cardiff rugby union side that included nine Welsh internationals. Peter West's commentary on the tourists' 6-5 success had formed the backbone of that afternoon's edition of *Grandstand*.

As brave and notable an effort as this was by the Cardiff XV, the attention of pretty much the whole world was focused on Texas where, the previous day, President John F. Kennedy had succumbed to an assassin's bullets as the presidential motorcade made its way through the Dallas streets.

It was against this shocking backdrop that BBC1 transmitted the very first episode of a new science fiction series: *Doctor Who*. Nearly four and a half million viewers tuned in to watch what would become a momentous piece of television history; although few could have realized at the time.

Those twenty-three-and-a-bit black-and-white minutes were used to introduce viewers to the new characters and give just a taste of the alien background of the eponymous Doctor and Susan—the Coal Hill School pupil who lived with her grandfather inside the 76 Totter's Lane scrapyard nominally owned by I. M. Foreman.

Two teachers from Coal Hill School, Barbara Wright and Ian Chesterton, were intrigued by Susan's remarkable historical and scientific knowledge, yet every bit as baffled by her apparent ignorance of contemporary life. Their curiosity led them to the seemingly disused junkyard and an encounter with an eccentric elderly gentleman outside an old police telephone box.

Hearing Susan's voice, Barbara rushed inside the telephone box, to be met by the sight of a futuristic console in the middle of a room that was incomprehensibly much larger than implied by external dimensions.

The Doctor didn't take kindly to the uninvited intrusion, and concerned that his "secret" would be revealed if the teachers left the police box (no seriously, it's a spacecraft), he locked the doors and transported the occupants back to prehistoric times.

The actual episode that was broadcast that Saturday evening was not the only edit of "An Unearthly Child." Several other versions still exist, and the various untransmitted takes are commonly and collectively known as "The Pilot Episode."

One adaptation was shown on television during the summer of 1991, and another edit has been made available as part of BBC DVD releases. Depending on which particular version you watch, there are a number of production errors and, in addition, several dialogue and costume changes were made prior to the recording of the episode that was finally transmitted. Some of the mistakes and problems are as follows:

Ian and Barbara struggled to open the door into a classroom where Susan was dancing to a song being played on her radio. It's not possible to see exactly what prevented them from entering the room, but the delay meant that Susan's mystical dance had to continue slightly longer than planned. The music was by John Smith and the Common Men, and Susan told Ian that the song had gone "from two to nineteen in the hit parade," before correcting herself and reversing the numbers.

Whilst sitting in a car outside the scrapyard, Ian's face was almost totally obscured by shadow due to poor work by the lighting department, and once inside the junkyard, two things fell to the floor: Ian's torch (intended) and, rather noisily, a shop mannequin (unintended). There was also a problem with the doors to the craft—which Susan revealed was known by the acronym TARDIS: "time and relative dimensions in space"—which, at one point, opened and clattered against the scenery. Unusually the disruption was enough to cause the whole scene to be abandoned and rerecorded.

From the continuity aspect, the outfit that Susan was wearing inside the TARDIS changed, as to a certain extent did her demeanor. In the pilot, she was dressed in a futuristic costume and was depicted as being more mature than her school age would have suggested.

Producers were keen to make Susan's character more readily identifiable to the younger members of the audience and so, to that end, amendments were made both to the script and to Susan's clothes, which were changed to a more contemporary pair of trousers and striped top.

Probably the most notable of the dialogue revisions had Susan stating she was born "in another time, another world," whereas in the pilot she had been "born in the forty-ninth century." Rather than simply being from the future, Susan's alien origins were made much clearer.

And so, with a few wheezes and clanks, the TARDIS dematerialized, and after bidding farewell to the cavemen, the crew arrived on Skaro for a classic first encounter with the Daleks.

Although there were quite a few history-based stories in the program's formative years, it was surely the monsters that really gripped the imagination. The Doctor's deadliest adversaries made a dramatic entrance at the end of the first episode of "The Dead Planet." Right across the country, children shielded their eyes in genuine terror as parents agreed it was really about time they got round to unblocking that sink.

The formula of a machine that bore no resemblance to the human form, spoke with a grating, emotionless voice, and showed neither remorse for its actions nor care for the wellbeing of any other species, well it was always likely to be a winner, and so it proved. Huge audiences tuned in to see the Doctor overcome the Dalek threat, in a story that essentially marked the creation of a television phenomenon.

As the first season progressed, so the main characters developed and the mistrust with which the Doctor had initially viewed his human companions gradually faded. A two-parter entitled "The Edge of Destruction" was filmed entirely inside the TARDIS, and it afforded the opportunity for some meaningful interaction between the quartet, without the intervention of some enemy intent on universal domination.

Next came a meeting with the famous explorer Marco Polo. Obviously it wasn't the real Marco Polo; in fact, on closer inspection, it turned out to be none other than Alan Bradley from *Corrie*—and the news was that the Weatherfield bad boy was intent on giving the Doctor's TARDIS to the emperor Kublai Khan.

The story ran for seven episodes, but a whole lot of time and money could have been saved if there had been Blackpool trams back in the thirteenth century. Coincidentally, William Russell (who portrayed Ian Chesterton) would later join the cast of *Coronation Street* to play Ted Sullivan, yet another love interest (in fact short-lived husband) of Rita.

Anyway, the remainder of that opening season alternated between science fiction adventures and historical tales; clearly the presence of two (albeit fictional) teachers provided a link with those elements of the program that were intended to be—to a greater or lesser degree—educational. Ian and Barbara's reaction to so many new situations must have helped to draw in the viewer, as the pair were essentially the eyes of the audience as they stepped out onto alien terrain, or came face-to-face with a famous name from times gone by.

The four main protagonists returned for a second season, and it wasn't long before the Daleks reappeared... on Earth, in 2164.

The story had two stand-out moments for me: the first (although chronologically the second) was Susan's decision to remain on Earth with a newfound love in the shape of resistance fighter David Campbell.

With the Dalek menace defeated, the time traveling Doctor realized that his granddaughter had fallen for the young Scot, but he was also aware that Susan would always put her grandfather's wellbeing ahead of her own happiness. Therefore, the Doctor locked the TARDIS doors, leaving Susan outside and effectively forcing her hand. The scene was incredibly poignant as the Doctor said farewell: "One day, I shall come back. Yes, I shall come back. Until then, there must be no regrets, no tears, no anxieties. Just go forward in all your beliefs and prove to me that I am not mistaken in mine. Goodbye, my dear. Goodbye, Susan."

Not a dry eye. Brilliant stuff.

The other moment was an iconic Dalek entrance. If the sight of malevolent mechanoids trundling through the English capital wasn't incongruous enough, the sequence in which a Dalek emerged from the murky waters of the River Thames was nothing short of inspired but...

And it's a big "but"...

Here is the moment where this final edition of the book veers away from its predecessors. If I could put into words the sounds of a drum roll and trumpet fanfare, now would be the time. Sadly I can't, and therefore you're just going to have to use your imagination, but....

I found Susan Foreman!!!

After, let's just say, "several" attempts to contact Carole Ann Ford over a period spanning more than two and a half years, this picture was nudged through my letterbox in December 2012. Some companions may have continued to prove elusive, but to eventually receive a reply from the lady whose character inspired the title of the book was a lovely moment.

Carole Ann Ford was born in June 1940. She had always wanted to be on stage and was a natural performer. She suffered a bout of pneumonia when she was eleven, which ended her hopes of becoming a dancer, but Carole Ann progressed into acting and made a string of appearances in well-known television series such as *Emergency Ward*

Carole Ann Ford

10, *Dixon of Dock Green*, and *Z-Cars*, as well as a small role in the 1962 film *The Day of the Triffids*.

Then, in March 1963, she played the part of Jacky in an episode of the *Suspense* series, entitled "The Man on the Bicycle," and her performance was apparently instrumental in her being offered the role of Susan Foreman.

In a 2010 interview, Carole Ann revealed:

> "The Edge of Destruction" was my favorite story to act in. Scripts varied, some brilliant, some not so good, but mostly frustrating for me, as they were rather repetitive.
>
> ... It was my choice to leave. My character was getting rather boring, she was never really developed. I don't think they knew what to do with me [although] I would rather have gone on a more upbeat note rather than for "true love."

Susan's departure paved the way for the arrival of Vicki, a traveler from Earth, whose spaceship had crashed on the planet Dido. She joined the crew after the "death" of fellow survivor Bennett—who was actually masquerading as a sinister spiky-faced creature named Koquillion—and, after a trip back to ancient Rome, the TARDIS landed on the planet Vortis to be greeted by various alien species, including the insect-like Zarbi.

This particular story ("The Web Planet") must have proved difficult for parents across the country as, far from being terrified, I presume the kids would have been asking exactly what some bloke was doing with his legs dangling out of a ridiculous ant costume.

Over thirteen million viewers tuned in to watch the opening episode—the highest individual total during the 1960s—but, just seven days later, that number had reduced by one million—quite probably because the "monsters" were so unrealistic.

Curiously, "The Web Planet" is regarded as the first and only story set outside the TARDIS to feature no humanoid characters apart from the Doctor and his companions. I suppose the knobbly-kneed Zarbi didn't count then.

Digression time now: The sixth and final installment of "The Web Planet" (entitled "The Centre") aired on March 20, 1965, and coincided with the Eurovision Song Contest, which was held in Naples. Luxembourg emerged victorious, with the winning song "Poupée de cire, poupée de son" ("wax doll, sawdust doll") being performed by the seventeen-year-old France Gall. The song is my all-time musical guilty pleasure, so if you're looking for any connection with *Doctor Who*, there isn't one, save for the fact that France Gall was very pretty indeed, and she would probably have made the perfect foil for the Doctor . . . had the series been French—*Docteur Qui*.

Nipping back to Rome, the next photo is the one I received from Maureen O'Brien, who played Vicki (left—the late Jacqueline Hill as Barbara Wright is on the right).

Maureen was born in Liverpool in June 1943, and her incredibly varied career has included work on television, radio, and in the theatre—she has also directed as well as running acting workshops. As if that wasn't enough, her writing skills have developed from a play on the London stage to a string of crime novels, which feature the character Detective Inspector John Bright.

Anyway, Vicki was still with the Doctor when the TARDIS arrived on the planet Xeros for what was an absolutely superb opening to "The Space Museum." The premise of the four-part story revolved around whether the future was predetermined or able to be changed, and this was excellently realized in a challenging first episode, which included a number of events, or clues which led towards the cliff hanger.

Maureen O'Brien (left) and Jacqueline Hill

First of all, whilst still inside the TARDIS, Vicki dropped a glass of water that then shattered on the floor . . . only for it to promptly "unshatter"—I wasn't sure of the best word—and jump back into her hand. However, I would have to question the absurdly complicated contraption needed to get the water: How can a spaceship have the technology to travel through time and space yet not have a tap?

After landing on Xeros, the absence of footprints on the sandy surface was soon noticed, and the mystery deepened when two of the ruling Moroks passed by, literally a few feet away, yet were completely oblivious to the fact that Vicki had sneezed . . . loudly. Inside the museum, the crew ended up equally close to a group of black-clad strangers who were talking, although no sound could be heard—my guess is that they were planning on delivering some Milk Tray.

Vicki then discovered she could put her hand straight through an inanimate exhibit, before the foursome eventually saw the shocking sight of themselves encased as museum pieces.

The truth was that the TARDIS had arrived on a different time track, and events therefore appeared out of synch. The crew saw their future before it happened and realized that once the exhibits disappeared, the timelines would have caught up; they would become both real and visible and would then have to set about trying to avoid ending up as curiosities in a museum.

This creates a really intriguing paradox. If you purposely do things in a certain way to prevent an unwanted outcome, do you simply take the path that leads directly to your intended fate anyway?

This basic theme is genuinely thought-provoking, but sadly, despite the TARDIS regulars being on pretty good form throughout, the plot weakened and the story simply fell away amid some dire performances from members of the supporting cast. Maybe the underlying philosophy was considered too much for a younger audience, but if that was the case, why bother with the story—especially episode one—at all?

Ian and Barbara remained with the Doctor until a 1965 romp called "The Chase," which involved the TARDIS crew being . . . er . . . chased by the Daleks.

This was the end of the line for the two human companions, as they used a Dalek time machine to return back to their home planet. The adventure also signaled the arrival of new companion Steven Taylor, played by the future *Blue Peter* presenter Peter Purves. The chase concept was weak and the adventure far from memorable as a result, although the appearance of The Beatles—albeit on video—performing *Ticket to Ride* is worthy of mention—as is Ian's ability to sing the chorus of a song recorded two years *after* he'd left Earth!

As for Jacqueline Hill, she spent some time raising a family after her stint on the program, but returned to acting in the late 1970s. She actually reappeared in *Doctor Who*, taking the part of Lexa in the Tom Baker story *Meglos* in 1980, but sadly Jacqueline died (of cancer) in 1993.

Reasonably soon after Ian and Barbara's departure, Vicki decided to remain in ancient Troy, having fallen in love with a prince named Troilus. Katarina (Adrienne Hill) joined the crew, but met a fairly swift demise in the very next story, "The Daleks Master Plan," which also featured the brief appearance of Sara Kingdom (Jean Marsh), who suffered an equally quick, but particularly gruesome, end at the hands of the Time Destructor, which aged her body and turned it into ash.

In the twelve-parter, "Dusty" Kingdom's brother, Brett Vyon, was played by Nicholas Courtney, who would become a familiar face on *Doctor Who* as Brigadier (as well as other ranks) Alistair Lethbridge-Stewart.

At the end of a story entitled "The Massacre," Dorothea Chaplet (Jackie Lane) entered the TARDIS, genuinely believing it to be a police telephone box. She was known as "Dodo," and it didn't take long to work out why, as she seemed happy to befriend anyone who was liable to kill her.

In "The Celestial Toymaker," Steven and Dodo had to compete in, and win, a series of games against living characters created from inanimate objects by the sheer power of the Toymaker's will. With the lives of the TARDIS crew at stake, Dodo's sympathetic nature did little to lessen the peril of the situations in which she was placed, culminating in a lethal dice game against the horrible schoolboy Cyril, whose incessant attempts at cheating didn't fool Steven, but worked every time on the hapless Dodo.

Eventually, Cyril literally fell victim to one of his own ruses: slipping on powder left for the travelers and tumbling to his death on an electrified floor.

Dodo's farewell came later in 1966, in "The War Machines," set in modern-day London—for the first time in the series' history. She was "replaced" by secretary Polly (Anneke Wills) and her new sailor friend Ben Jackson (played by the late Michael Craze). I've got a couple of nice little sidelines to that story, both of which appeared in the book's earlier incarnations, but in fairness I think they're pretty decent sidelines and deserve to retain their place within these pages.

Firstly, episode four included a very early appearance of stand-up comedian and actor Mike Reid. He played the part of a soldier who was presumably being given the *Runaround* by the metallic machines.

And secondly, the story featured an actor with one of those faces you recognize but that you just can't put a name to. The gentleman in question was William Mervyn, better known as the kindly passenger who always waved at the Waterbury children from his seat in the rear carriage of the train in the 1970 movie *The Railway Children*.

In the film, the sisters Roberta and Phyllis were played by Jenny Agutter and Sally Thomsett respectively. Phyllis was supposed to be eleven years old, but Sally Thomsett was born in 1950, making her twenty when the film was released. She was contractually banned from revealing her true age and also from driving, drinking, or smoking during filming. The irony is, whilst Roberta was several years older than Phyllis, Jenny Agutter was actually born in 1952, making her younger than her younger sister . . . if you see what I mean!

As a brief aside to the sideline: Anneke Wills—newly installed as Polly—had played the part of Roberta in a 1957 television adaptation of E. Nesbit's novel.

Anyway, Ben and Polly became the first companions to witness a Time Lord regeneration, as William Hartnell transformed into Patrick Troughton at the end of "The Tenth Planet" —a defining point in the program's history.

Almost as worthy of comment though, was the moment in episode four when Michael Craze (as Ben) shouted: "We save their grotty plonet Mandos for what?" (instead of "planet Mondas"), to prove that Hartnell didn't have a monopoly in the line-fluffing department.

The adventure featured the first ever appearance of the silver giants, the Cybermen, who would become regular foes for many subsequent incarnations of the Doctor. Whilst the costumes may not have been perfect, the effect—helped by the story's polar setting—must have been chilling indeed—no pun intended. Perhaps the most unsettling aspect of this particular Cyberman was the voice. Although future helmet designs would essentially have a slit for a mouth, the original had a moveable mouth that formed an "o" shape when speaking. Lines were delivered with an exaggerated inflection on what we would consider the wrong syllable of a word. The result was a kind of musical-type intonation that was close enough to human speech to reflect inhabitants of a former twin planet, yet far enough removed to feel both alien and threatening.

Incidentally, back in the mid-1970s, I purchased—as a proud member of the Doctor Who Appreciation Society—a C120 cassette containing audio recordings of the final episode of the first three Doctor's respective tenures (viz. "The Tenth Planet," "The War Games," and "Planet of the Spiders") and the very first episode of Tom Baker's opening story, "Robot." The tape was played over and over again, and I am actually quite proud to admit that I knew the Cybermen's lines word for word and could repeat them using my own special pubescent random voice-breaking intonation.

Obviously, many years have passed since then, the voice is much deeper now—but strangely soothing I'm led to believe—and although the cassette met its demise as a tangled mess in the tape recorder a long time ago, I can—thanks to audio CD—still listen to the final installment of "The Tenth Planet" —arguably the most sought-after of all the "missing" *Doctor Who* episodes—and yes, I can still remember the words. Sad but impressive in equal measures.

But I digress. Earlier in the story, there was the slightly worrying scene as Earth's twin planet was viewed for the first time, and those gathered in front of the image of Mondas thought it looked vaguely familiar: "Hey Ben," exclaimed Polly, "that bit looks just like . . . Malaysia!"

Sorry?! Malaysia?!!

Now of all the land masses this planet has to offer, I'd be willing to bet a considerable amount of money that the first country I'd identify wouldn't be Malaysia—it wouldn't be the second . . . nor the third for that matter. In fact, the only people in with a real chance of recognizing the outline of this particular country would have been glued to a television set somewhere in or near Kuala Lumpur.

Into episode two and, luckily for all of us, a picture of Mondas had been taken from Mount Palomar observatory and the news presenter said: "Some observers have reported that its land masses resemble those of Earth, but this is being hotly disputed in top astronomical circles and no general agreement has yet been reached."

Now I'm no scientist—although I do have a Physics 'O' level—but if you simply rotated the image of Mondas by one hundred and eighty degrees you got . . . Earth!

If only I'd been born a few years earlier, I would, by definition, have moved in those "top astronomical circles," but it's more than a slight concern that the world was trying to defeat a race of giant silver killing machines, yet the best minds we had to offer couldn't flip over a picture.

Hang on a second Polly. Isn't that Java?

CHALLENGE ANNEKE

So enter Patrick Troughton; in my opinion the actor whose portrayal of the Doctor defines the role.

Of all the traits he brought to the part, it was his ability to appear flustered, yet be able to manipulate or control a situation that stood out—to be the proverbial one step ahead—and there are aspects of Matt Smith's performance that are certainly reminiscent—to me at least—of Troughton.

Along with Ben and Polly, Jamie McCrimmon (Frazer Hines) soon joined the fold after the TARDIS visited Scotland at the time of the Battle of Culloden, and for me—yet again—the character of Jamie embodied the ideal male companion for the Doctor. The fact that he was plucked from the relative obscurity of eighteenth century Earth allowed the writers to reveal the sheer wonderment of space and time travel through Jamie's innocent eyes.

The young Scot was in no position to comprehend the technical advances to which he was exposed, nor the alien beings he encountered, yet Jamie possessed enough bravery, loyalty, and chivalry to cope with almost every situation, and even if he didn't completely understand the full extent of the many dangers the crew faced, he readily accepted the role of physical protector.

That said, writing scripts for four main characters would have presented a number of challenges and, on balance, the format and flow of the show does seem to work better when there are only one or two companions.

Anyway, next up was a dire offering entitled "The Underwater Menace," which was set . . . oh, you guessed. The good news is that the story does not exist in its entirety; the bad news is that in late 2011, episode two was discovered—episode three was already in the archives. The initial excitement of unearthing an episode previously assumed to have been lost must have disappeared almost instantly, to be replaced with a temptation to hide the tape and walk away, whistling innocently and pretending you'd never seen it. On the upside, episode three of the William Hartnell adventure "Galaxy 4" was also discovered via the same source—a former television engineer named Terry Burnett.

Whilst "The Underwater Menace" is pretty desperate stuff, it does feature a strong contender for the "Deluded Mad Scientist of the Season" award, in the shape of Professor Zaroff—he of the false-sounding eastern European accent that was seemingly actor Joseph Furst's natural voice. At the end of episode three, Zaroff screamed: "Nothing in ze vorld can stop me now!"

Oh I think you'll find it can Professor.

Thankfully the Cybermen made a swift return in the 1967 story "The Moonbase." Sadly—on this occasion—only two of the four episodes survive, but they include a really good cliff hanger at the end of episode two, when a fruitless search for the Cybermen's hiding place ended with the group in the sick bay: "Did your men search in here? "

"Did they? Did they search in here?!" whispered the Doctor.

Anneke Wills

The answer was "no," and even though that could only mean there was a Cyberman lying under a sheet on one of the beds, it was still a scary moment when the covers were thrown aside and a menacing giant climbed off the bed—nearly knocking it over in the process—before advancing on the Doctor, Polly, and base commander Hobson.

The next adventure, "The Faceless Ones," is not only the focus of the next part of this lengthy chapter but it is also my favorite ever *Doctor Who* story and marks the final appearances of both Michael Craze and Anneke

Wills—who both chose to stay in London on what turned out to be the same day they had originally left. And now would seem to be an opportune moment to include one of the photos I received from Anneke as long ago as June 2010.

More recently—in February 2013 to be precise—I had the chance to e-mail Anneke one or two questions about her time in *Doctor Who*. I tried really hard to think up questions that were insightful as opposed to generic, but when the reply to one four-liner was two words—and no, the second one wasn't "off!"—I realized that my all-too-brief career as a serious interviewer was officially over.

Before I return to the subject in hand, I did wonder how it had felt to have been involved in a series that had undergone what was the relative uncertainty of a change of leading actor:

"Now, fifty years on (or so!), we can look back and have lots of opinions about it, but at the time Mike [*Craze*] and I just felt relieved Bill [*Hartnell*] was leaving, excited that Patrick Troughton was joining us and anxious that our work would continue!"

As far as "The Faceless Ones" is concerned, I guess you could pick holes in almost any television script from that era—if you were so inclined—but sometimes the words put into the mouths of certain characters are almost ridiculous.

For example, in episode one, a police officer was zapped by Spencer using a futuristic ray gun, and from the point of view of effective killing, you would have to say "job done." But when it came to disposing of the Doctor, Jamie, and Samantha in episode four, Spencer opted for the unnecessarily elaborate *Goldfinger*-style laser demise rather than the triple zap that he initially considered, which surely would have worked given the fact that the three intended victims were lying paralyzed on the floor.

Yet in episode six, the Chameleon Director (in the form of Detective Inspector Crossland) arrogantly declared: "We are the most intelligent race in the universe."

Er, no you're not!

And the fact that the Chameleon creatures never returned to face the Time Lord again suggests that the embodiment of their threat may not have been particularly well received. Yet the concept of a race capable of assuming human form and characteristics is chilling indeed, and it was an idea that had already—and successfully—reached the big screen, courtesy of the 1956 film *Invasion of the Body Snatchers*.

Science fiction's readily identifiable monster was now a friend, a neighbor, or even a close family member, and for the viewer to imagine themselves in the situation the characters are facing is unnerving to say the least.

Irrational behavior demands a rational explanation, but how can that be forthcoming when the reality of an alien invasion is the last thing an ordinary person in an ordinary situation would be expecting? But that is the essence of this kind of story: abnormal normality—or should that be the other way around?

Chronologically, "The Faceless Ones" (originally entitled "The Chameleons") was the thirty-fifth *Doctor Who* adventure and was given the series code "KK." The first William Hartnell adventure was coded "A," and the subsequent stories followed the alphabet—with the exception of the letter "I." The letters were doubled from story twenty-six and so on.

"The Faceless Ones" was jointly written by Malcolm Hulke and David Ellis. Hulke (1924-1979) was a noted television writer, his credits including episodes of *Target Luna, The Avengers, The Protectors* and, perhaps slightly surprisingly, *Crossroads*. *The Avengers* 1962 episode entitled "The Mauritius Penny," was written by Hulke and adapted for television by Terrance Dicks. The pair also collaborated in Troughton's final romp, "The War Games," before penning several further stories during the Jon Pertwee era between 1970 and 1974.

David Ellis—who died in 1978—had written for *Dixon of Dock Green* and *Z Cars*. He had seen several scripts for *Doctor Who* rejected, but it was a joint effort with Hulke in "The Big Store" that would eventually be reworked into "The Faceless Ones."

Hulke had later recalled:

Both being writers, we [Hulke and Ellis] started telling each other stories. I put up an idea —nothing to do with Doctor Who—he elaborated on it and we decided to work it out together. So we collaborated over the next few weeks and worked out a film story, which we never sold.

Then I think it was David who said 'Why don't you and I have a stab at Doctor Who?' As I'd written for the series before, we got in touch with Gerry Davis. We discussed it with him and he said he would like a story set in a big department store. So we worked out a story called "The Big Store," in which the Chameleons posed as shop dummies. Gerry was quite pleased with this, but then the producer said 'Big stores are out, try an airport!'

So we started again and the final story came out of that.

The basic synopsis of "The Big Store" involved the TARDIS materializing in a department store in England in 1973, where the crew encountered a group of aliens intent on conquering and colonizing Earth by releasing a virulent strain of bubonic plague. The aliens consisted of two distinct groups: a highly intelligent master race and a class of faceless, mindless servants, able to assume the external characteristics of human beings.

The first episode's cliff hanger was due to involve Polly admiring the store's range of seventies' fashions when, in a mirror, she saw one of the shop dummies walking towards her, its hands reaching for her throat.

The concept of humanoid facsimiles and the sight of mannequins coming to life would be seen in Jon Pertwee's first adventure, "Spearhead from Space," in which creatures dressed as shop dummies smashed through shop windows to signal the start of the Auton invasion.

Anneke Wills

Back in 1967, however, the production team had requested a change in this story's setting for the simple reason that they had recently been granted permission to do some filming at Gatwick Airport. This really was a major coup for the program. The location work added very real scale to the production, and director Gerry Mill made full use of the terminal building and those runway areas where the crew was allowed to shoot.

As has been mentioned, this adventure was notable for signaling the departures of Ben and Polly, and the signed picture of Anneke on the previous page is actually a screen shot from her farewell story.

Michael Craze and Anneke Wills were both contracted to appear until the second episode of "Evil of the Daleks," but although the BBC paid up their contracts in full, both were written out at the end of "The Faceless Ones." In fact, they disappeared from the action fairly early on in the story and only reappeared in the final episode's closing moments—in a pre-filmed sequence—to say their farewells to the Doctor and Jamie.

I have read varying accounts regarding their departures. Malcolm Hulke is quoted as saying: "The producer had rather gone off them as actor and actress, I recall." Having had to rework the script once to change the setting from shop to airport, Hulke and Ellis were then faced with making further amendments to write out two of the main characters.

This is how Anneke herself described how her time on *Doctor Who* drew to a close: "I remember that they approached Mike to tell him they were writing him out—did I want to stay or go? Partly out of loyalty to Mike and partly because I was afraid of being typecast, I chose to leave as well."

Their departure was simplified from the point of view of continuity by the story's modern-day setting. Although *Doctor Who*'s first episode "An Unearthly Child" started in London during 1963, "The Faceless Ones" was only the second full adventure to take place on contemporary Earth.

The other occasion—as mentioned in the previous chapter—was "The War Machines," and although "The Faceless Ones" was transmitted just under a year later, the action supposedly ended on exactly the same date, meaning that the second Doctor was battling the Chameleons and returning Ben and Polly to Earth at pretty much the same time as the first incarnation was pitting his wits against WOTAN before dematerializing with Ben and Polly on board the TARDIS.

This left Jamie as the sole companion for most of the story, although he befriended Samantha Briggs (Pauline Collins), the sister of one of the kidnapped teenagers. It had been hoped that Samantha might become a permanent addition to the series, but Innes Lloyd was unable to persuade Pauline Collins to extend her stay.

Anyway, that's enough background: time for the dreaded review. What first struck me about "The Faceless Ones" was the length of the story. I read somewhere that the original script was a four-part adventure, and the fact that it was ultimately extended to six episodes implies a fair amount of padding to fill out the extra forty-five to fifty minutes.

There are a number of occasions when this becomes apparent. For me, the start of episodes two to six repeats far more of the previous installment's cliff hanger than is really necessary and this is, to a certain extent, just wasted time. The early episodes are littered with captures and escapes, but the most criminal piece of padding is the elaborate laser beam death trap, which I referred to earlier.

Unfortunately, such incidents take away credibility from the Chameleon's repeated claims that they are a race of unparalleled intelligence. Their leader, the Director, refuses to believe that the human originals have been located back on Earth, even when Chameleon Jenkins simply dissolves in front of him. The Chameleon's plight may arguably be deserving of some measure of sympathy, however, even if you wave away the kidnappings as misguided, there can be no excuse for the murders of, firstly, Inspector Gascoigne, then the RAF pilot, and finally, at the hands of Chameleon Nurse Pinto, the policeman.

If their race is as ruthless at those killings would suggest, they accept their eventual fate with a surprising lack of resistance; the Director is shot and killed by one of his own (Chameleon Blade), who is clearly only concerned with self-preservation. The Doctor tells the airport Commandant that Blade can now be trusted—the viewer may not have been quite so convinced.

At least Captain Blade gets to deliver one of the best lines of the whole story, when a captive Crossland warns of the "long arm of the British law."

"I don't think it'll reach where you're going," came the reply. Comedy or threat, they are both delivered with the same marvelous icy arrogance.

Whilst the story's concept was clearly not original, the fact that it was combined with a rare visit by the Doctor to contemporary Earth does add an extra element of tension and a welcome contrast to the customary monster-filled tales—especially following the demise of the series' historical adventures after "The Highlanders".

The processed Chameleons are sinister at times, and the raw-state creatures quite creepy—their true form not being immediately revealed, and the body-swapping scenes in the Medical Centre must have been quite scary for the younger members of the audience.

There is an implication that the arrival of the Chameleon Tours operation must have been relatively recent, otherwise it is difficult to explain why only one person (Samantha) is suspicious enough to come to Gatwick Airport and enquire as to the whereabouts of one solitary passenger in amongst the fifty thousand that had been taken.

However, given the facts that their "final flight of the season" is due for take-off and there are only eight scheduled flights per day, it would surely have taken a fair length of time to transfer so many people, and this makes Samantha's lone mission appear rather implausible.

I know that it had been hoped that Samantha would become a regular companion for the Doctor (and Jamie), but the character did come across as rather headstrong and talkative. If I was to give the benefit of the doubt, perhaps her manner was influenced by the desire to find her missing brother, but I think that the introduction of Victoria (from 1866) was a much better idea than simply replacing two modern-day companions with another.

Obviously with four of the six episodes still missing, it is hard to judge the overall success of both the internal and external filming, but due in part to the non-appearance of Ben and Polly, Jamie gets plenty of opportunity to come to terms with technology that's centuries ahead of his time.

From the initial shock at the sight of the "flying beasties," Jamie eventually pinches Samantha's plane ticket and travels up to the Chameleon space station to try and discover what fate has befallen the missing passengers. Despite the constant challenges of all things futuristic (in relative terms), Jamie shows himself to be sensible and adaptable—and his bravery and loyalty can never be doubted.

As for the Doctor, this story displays many of what I consider to be the strengths of the character. Patrick Troughton's Doctor always had the ability to play the fool and not only get people to unwittingly do exactly what he wanted but also lull his enemies into a false sense of security. With his mixture of childlike playfulness and unquestionable authority, the Doctor may have appeared mad to the Commandant at the start of the adventure, but by the end he trusted the Doctor implicitly.

The Commandant (played by Colin Gordon) is the sort of stereotypical authority figure that flatly refuses to believe in anything he doesn't understand or considers irrational. Clent (Peter Barkworth) in "The Ice Warriors" and Hobson (Patrick Barr) in "The Moonbase" are other examples from Troughton's era: "Stop this Cyberman nonsense. There were Cybermen, every child knows that, but they were all destroyed ages ago...." Hobson ("The Moonbase" episode two).

This creates a kind of recurring theme that the Doctor not only has to overcome an impending alien threat but also convince a skeptical mind of the danger that is about to be faced.

I just need to slot in a quick digression here—the part of the Commandant's assistant, Jean Rock, in "The Faceless Ones" was played by Wanda Ventham. This was the first of her three appearances in *Doctor Who* (the others being "Image of the Fendahl" and "Time and the Rani"). Wanda featured in a couple of *Carry On* films in the 1960s, she was also Col. Virginia Lake in *UFO*, and, more recently, she played Cassandra's mother, Pamela Parry, in *Only Fools and Horses*.

Wanda is the mother of actor Benedict Cumberbatch—and she also signed this screen shot from "The Faceless Ones" for me.

Wanda Ventham

Meanwhile, back in outer space... the Doctor's plan depends entirely on those left on Earth finding the human originals of their Chameleon counterparts, yet despite this he shows unwavering confidence in being able to outwit the Director and his fellow Chameleon replicas.

Perhaps the Doctor is helped by the fact that the Director has an over-inflated opinion of his own intelligence—or he underestimates the Doctor... or both. But in what is at times a nail-biting adventure with excellent cliff hangers—especially the apparent disappearance of all the plane passengers at the end of episode three—there is no doubt that the urgency of finding the missing human originals leads to a tense period in the final episode.

However, the conclusion of the story seems to be reached very quickly, although allowing his adversaries to simply leave is an interesting twist. We are left with Ben and Polly's farewell, which is quite a poignant moment. But arriving back on exactly the same day as they had originally left with the Doctor? You couldn't make it up!

All in all I would say that despite its obvious flaws, "The Faceless Ones" is a bit of a departure for *Doctor Who* in a number of ways. The surviving episodes, along with the audio recording and stills from the missing parts, suggest that the story worked. But, "The Faceless Ones" is always likely to be overlooked, possibly because only two episodes still exist, but more likely because the disappearance of the TARDIS at the end of the adventure led straight into what is considered an all-time classic story.

But for now, I will close with a little bit more from Anneke Wills. Did she feel that the dynamic of Ben and Polly was affected by the introduction of a third companion?

"It didn't seem at the time to alter anything much—more to join the party! Although the writers found it difficult, so Kit Pedler simply had Jamie conked out in a hospital bed most of the time!"

And if one of her "junked" adventures was found, which would she like to see again? "'The Smugglers'—it was both mine and Mike's favorite story."

Finally, a two-part question: what did Anneke feel that the character of Polly brought to the series, and if she could have played any other companion, who would it be? *Probing stuff eh?!*

"I think that Polly brought a bit of 1960s style fresh air; she was feisty, stylish and bright.

"Perhaps I would have liked to play Rose... then I could have worked with the wonderful David Tennant—and even kiss him!"

DAYLIGHT COME... TIME TO GO HOME

Back in 1967, the next story—if you hadn't guessed—was "Evil of the Daleks," in which the Doctor and Jamie were lured back to Victorian England where they once again came face to face—or face to eye stalk—with Skaro's finest.

The one surviving episode (the second) suggests an intriguing and atmospheric tale, but as is so often the case with the incomplete Troughton stories, the viewer is simply left wanting more. However, this little escapade did serve to introduce Deborah Watling as Victoria Waterfield, and many consider her era to be one of the series' golden periods—even though it only spanned six stories.

This probably has plenty to do with the adversaries that she encountered: Daleks, Yeti (twice), Ice Warriors, and Cybermen. But the latter were a fairly essential part of "The Tomb of the Cybermen," which is the sole adventure featuring Victoria where all the episodes are known to be in existence—although prints of this four-part tale were only discovered in Hong Kong as recently as 1991.

Without complete visual proof, judgments are based on surviving clips, audio recordings, photo stills, and a fast-fading memory. But things were so much better back then, weren't they?!

Deborah Watling

In actual fact, "The Tomb of the Cybermen" is the earliest complete adventure from the whole Troughton era; it's not the worst story I've ever seen, but I would argue that it's not as good as many would have insisted in, say, 1990.

Dodgy accents apart, I do like the moment when Jamie attempts to open the giant door into the tomb. His efforts prove to be in vain, but only because his foot is placed right against the seemingly immovable, but actually very light, door!

I was also struck by the charming innocence of the orphan Victoria—resplendent in an incongruous 1960s dress—especially her opinion of the Cybermen: "Mercy! They must have been giants!" They still are Victoria—although I'm guessing the twenty-first century phrase to convey similar surprise may not be quite so quaint!

The furry menace of the Yeti was defeated twice: once in Tibet and then in the murky London Underground. The stories also featured the unseen Great Intelligence, which made a slightly belated return in the 2012 Christmas Special "The Snowmen"—with the nice touch of including an old map of the underground system for the more mature viewers. Victoria decided to settle in modern-day England at the end of "Fury from the Deep," a story that featured the iconic and chilling scene of Messrs Oak and Quill emitting poisonous gas from their open mouths to render Maggie Harris unconscious.

Deborah Watling

It was Maggie and her husband who eventually agreed to care for Victoria. She bid the Doctor and Jamie a final farewell before the TARDIS dematerialized without her. This picture is a still from the end of "Fury from the Deep" signed by Deborah Watling.

Deborah was born in January 1948; she comes from an acting family, and Doctor Who gave her the opportunity to perform alongside her father Jack, who played Professor Travers in the two Yeti stories, "The Abominable Snowmen" and "The Web of Fear."

TARDIS departures were usually swiftly followed by a new arrival, and one story after Victoria chose to leave the Doctor and Jamie, they were joined by Zoë Heriot (played by Wendy Padbury), a complete contrast to her nineteenth-century-born predecessor.

Zoë was an astrophysicist and mathematician: logical in the extreme, with a photographic memory. Basically, she was a "smarty pants"—toned down considerably for the younger readers. However, her remarkable knowledge failed to hide a lack of emotional and social awareness, but as well as being afforded plenty of opportunities to display her great intellect, Zoë's character was able to develop alongside her newfound friends.

Despite being so different in nature, Jamie and Zoë grew into one of the series' most endearing partnerships, although their time together (the last adventure of series five, "The Wheel in Space," and the whole of season six) was littered with some of the weaker stories of the Troughton era.

One exception though is "The Mind Robber," the unusual, surreal, yet compelling five-parter, which was broadcast in the autumn of 1968. This story was an interesting departure from the more recognized format because the alien weapon was the power of the brain as opposed to some ray gun or the like. It was also the first *Doctor Who* story that I can actually recall watching. (I would have been a couple of months past my fourth birthday when the opening episode was aired.)

What I particularly remembered was the noise made by the White Robots. The sound isn't easy to describe, but I would liken it to the grating that comes from my rapidly wearing hips whenever I try to do anything remotely athletic.

It wasn't until I saw the BBC DVD of the story that I could place the memory of the robots. It was certainly frightening at the time, and the adventure was still eminently watchable all those years later.

I'm a huge fan of trivia, and so, to rather selfishly satisfy my own thirst for useless information, I can tell you that Frazer Hines contracted chickenpox during filming of "The Mind Robber," hence the need for a swift rewrite of the script to allow Hamish Wilson (a genuine Scot) to briefly take on the role of Jamie. Also, Frazer Hines's brother Ian was one of the clockwork soldiers in the same story.

In truth, whilst the White Robots were quite scary—a fact I am able to confirm because my father was with me behind the sofa—there was one moment from the television of my youth that I found genuinely frightening, and whilst this is going to be an embarrassing revelation, sometimes there are things you just have to do.

Back in the day, I seem to recall that there were intermissions—occasional short features lasting perhaps only a minute or so in between programs. There was one in particular that involved a rabbit singing the *Banana Boat Song* (that's "Day-O" to you and me). What happened was that the viewer looked into an empty room and the opening line could be heard faintly in the distance. The sound of footsteps followed as the presumably Plasticine rabbit approached the closed door.

The singing became louder, the door opened, the rabbit entered and I started screaming and sobbing. It got me every time, and I've no idea why. I did mention it to my parents a couple of years ago; they could vaguely remember the rabbit, but they had clearly forgotten how badly traumatized their young son had been by the whole terrible ordeal.

Returning to Wendy Padbury, officially my "original" female companion. She was, at one time, married to Melvyn Hayes, who is probably best remembered for his portrayal of Bombardier "Gloria" Beaumont in the sitcom *It Ain't Half Hot Mum*. He had previously appeared as Albert in the kid's television series *Here Come the Double Deckers*, which revolved around the adventures of seven children whose den was an old red double-decker bus in a disused junkyard.

Amazing what you can find in a junkyard....

If you're wanting to know what relevance this has to *Doctor Who*, the answer is absolutely none at all, but the show—which ran for seventeen episodes between 1970 and 1971—featured Debbie Russ (who played Tiger) and she was my first ever crush. Debbie, whose character owned a fluffy tiger called... er... "Tiger," would have been ten years old at the time, and as I was only six going on seven, I doubt she would have looked at me twice. But a boy could dream couldn't he?!

Back in time and space, the Cybermen soon made another appearance, emerging from the London sewers in a bid to take over Earth. "The Invasion" ran for eight episodes, but the series finale "The War Games" lasted even longer—ten episodes in all.

It was hardly a surprise that plenty of to-and-fro, capture and escape-style padding was needed for such a saga, but much as the first nine parts had their tedious moments, the final episode was superb; the viewer was treated to some long-awaited background into the Time Lords, the Doctor's own people.

After standing trial for "interference," the Doctor was sentenced to exile on Earth, and following one last failed escape attempt, both Jamie and Zoë were returned to a moment shortly before they each began their travels with the Doctor. This made their departure even more touching. As the Time Lords erased both companions' memories of the Doctor—apart from their respective first meeting—and of each other, they were duly returned to their original time streams.

The Doctor was all too well aware that his young friends would essentially forget all their adventures, as well as their bond and friendship—a situation that was repeated to a degree in more recent times when Donna Noble's mind was wiped to prevent her being killed by a human-Time-Lord metacrisis (ahh, one of those . . .).

GAIL WARNING

The new decade witnessed the introduction of the third Doctor (Jon Pertwee) and the arrival of York-born actress Caroline John, who played Dr. Elizabeth ("Liz") Shaw. Liz was a scientist attached to UNIT (United Nations Intelligence Taskforce), an organization that would have a prominent role in the Earth-based stories that prevailed over the majority of seasons seven and eight.

I hadn't been able to make contact with Caroline prior to the release of the first edition of this book, but in February 2011 I received two signed photographs and a note apologizing for not having responded to my earlier request—a request she undoubtedly had never seen. I had read that Caroline was always very kind towards fans of the show, and so it proved.

Caroline asked if she could have a copy of one of the photos she'd returned as she hadn't seen this particular picture before. I duly sent the photo and by way of a reply, a lovely two-page handwritten letter soon followed.

Caroline John

It was actually an autographed photo of Caroline John that had been the inspiration for *Desperately Seeking Susan Foreman*, so the pictures and letters that I received from her obviously meant a lot to me.

The news of her passing on June 5, 2012, aged 71, came as a shock, and the review of "The Ambassadors of Death"—one of the four stories in which Caroline starred—which forms the next chapter, is now included as a tribute to her memory.

Back in 1970, the restriction of stories to one fixed point in time and space clearly presented writers with a few problems, but the Autons that appeared twice in Jon Pertwee's opening five adventures were certainly an excellent concept. Good enough, in fact, to be chosen to face Christopher Eccleston's Doctor when the series made its return to the small screen in March 2005.

Scary monsters are all well and good, but there is something inherently unnerving about familiar everyday objects not only becoming animate, but having the means to attack.

The plastic shop mannequins in "Spearhead from Space" (the opening story of season seven) were superbly realized, and I wonder how many kids glanced uneasily towards shop windows all those years ago, half expecting the display dummies to move. John Collier certainly wasn't the only window to watch.

Liz Shaw was not a typical companion. For one thing, she never actually "flew" in the TARDIS—usually a prerequisite for companion status—and her scientific knowledge almost put her on an equal footing with the Doctor; he was trying to come to terms with his new appearance and the fact that the secrets of time travel had been taken from him, so he couldn't leave even if he wanted to.

Caroline John was one of the older assistants; she was twenty-nine when she joined the program and her relative maturity again gave Liz a different outlook to some of the younger companions, and the relationship between the pair was totally believable.

However, the opportunity to enquire is always an essential ingredient of the Doctor's sidekick, and the character of Liz Shaw did not need to pose the questions that inquisitive young viewers would have been asking. And that may have been one of the main reasons why producer Barry Letts did not renew Caroline's contract.

Even if there had been an offer on the table, Caroline would not have returned, as she revealed in a wonderful 1999 "Wine and Dine" interview.

> The only person I'd told was my dresser, Jean . . . when I left it [the pregnancy] was about four and a half or five months. Some people get very big very quickly . . . but I didn't.
>
> I think it was at the end of 'Ambassadors' [of Death], in the studios and he [Barry Letts] came and said 'we're looking for somebody new'. He didn't know about me being pregnant, I was a bit shocked, but at the same time totally relieved.
>
> In hindsight though, I think it was in advance of its time and it's popular now because the woman isn't spoken down to. Other fans say they like Liz Shaw because she stands up to the Doctor . . . but [my departure was] valid at the time . . . they wanted a sort of bimbo character.
>
> I wouldn't actually have wanted to go on longer, because it might have ruined my career . . . I'd learned what I could, but I still think the [new] producer wanted to put his mark on [the program].

Here is the second signed photo that Caroline sent to me, and the review of my favorite of the four Liz Shaw stories follows immediately after the conclusion of this chapter.

Caroline John

The Doctor's new companion was Josephine "Jo" Grant, the daughter of a high-ranking civil servant who had pulled a string or two to get her a position within UNIT.

Jo was certainly enthusiastic and effervescent, but equally scatter-brained, and the Doctor was obviously disappointed that Jo was most definitely not an accomplished scientist like her predecessor. That said, Jo was warm and endearing, and the Doctor became particularly fond of his young assistant.

Katy Manning was given the part of Jo, despite what I have seen described as a "shambolic audition." Katy's infectious personality was instilled into Jo and combined with Jon Pertwee's all-action portrayal of the Time Lord, this period in the series' history proved extremely popular; audience figures rose steadily towards the ten million mark, after having nose-dived towards half that number at the end of Pertwee's first year in the role.

Their first adventure together featured another battle with the Autons, but this time, as well as dolls, objects such as plastic chairs and daffodils came to life with lethal consequences. The story was entitled "The Terror of the Autons" and introduced the Doctor's nemesis, a fellow renegade Time Lord known simply as the Master, who was originally portrayed by a sinister-looking Roger Delgado. The Master's arrival allowed plots to be widened from the constraints of the basic "aliens invade Earth" scenario.

By 1971, the TARDIS was back in use, as the Time Lords dispatched the Doctor and Jo to sort out an inter-planetary mining dispute. And there was one familiar face amongst the locals, that of Helen Worth, better known to many a soap addict as Gail (Potter, Tilsley, Platt, Hillman or McIntyre—take your pick) from *Coronation Street*.

Over the years, Gail has acquired quite a gift in the "most times I get close to a bloke, he seems to die" department, and if her character Mary had enjoyed similar powers, "Colony in Space" may have had a completely different outcome. In the event, she was able to help her people build their colony before returning to Earth and wreaking terrible revenge on the male population of Weatherfield (Lewis Archer apart, obviously).

I have already mentioned, in passing, the fact that William Russell and Mark Eden also appeared in *Doctor Who* before strolling down television's most famous cobbled street. Just to continue the theme, here are a few more who have appeared in both series down the years: Sarah Lancashire, Anne Reid, Peter Kay (believe it or not), and two members of the

Grimshaw family—Bruno Langley, who played Eileen's son Todd, went on to be cast as Adam Mitchell in the Christopher Eccleston story "Dalek," and Eileen's father Colin, who spent a few months in the soap from late 2008 to May 2009.

The role of Colin was filled by Edward de Souza who, many years earlier, had played the part of space agent Marc Cory in "Mission to the Unknown" (aka "Dalek Cutaway"). This was a single episode, which aired in 1965 that (uniquely) didn't include any of the regular characters but was intended to pave the way for "The Daleks Master Plan."

Although de Souza only managed a six-month stint in Weatherfield before succumbing to a heart attack, that was considerably longer than he survived in *Doctor Who*, as he was surrounded by Daleks and blasted into oblivion before the episode's twenty-five minutes were over.

Anyway, along with the fairly regular appearances of the Master, many stories from the Pertwee era were notable for the use of color separation overlay (CSO), also known as chroma key—the use of green, blue or yellow screens to add images to live action and give the appearance that the separate events are in the same shot. It's a belting idea in principle, but misalignment in the two recordings rendered the effects anything but "special" and the overlay was glaringly obvious at times.

Still, better to try and use the available technology I suppose; maybe it was budget limits or time constraints that meant the end result wasn't always convincing.

Bumbling bureaucrats were another regular feature, with the Doctor often battling an alien foe as well as the intransigence of officials who refused to accept threats that were staring them (sometimes literally) in the face.

That said, there were a couple of quite strong ideas spanning the end of season eight and the beginning of season nine (1971-72). Firstly there was "The Daemons," set in a village named Devil's End (sometimes there's a clue in the name), which was inhabited by a stone gargoyle that came to life and a giant hooved creature named Azal—which I always thought was toilet paper.

Swot alert: *a true stone-carved gargoyle has a water spout—if not, it is technically a "grotesque."*

Next, came "Day of the Daleks," in which a band of fanatical terrorists had traveled back in time with the intention of killing Sir Reginald Styles, a delegate at a peace conference. In the future, the world was ruled by the Daleks, and the guerrillas believed that the events leading to the planet's conquest could be traced back to an explosion for which they blamed Styles.

The Doctor eventually realized that the explosion was triggered accidentally by one of the terrorists whilst trying to carry out his mission. The temporal paradox of people from the future attempting to change events that they themselves caused—albeit inadvertently—is a really clever notion, but the story doesn't quite fulfill the promise of the idea, and that is mainly because of the lack of Daleks.

Now, I readily accept that as far as killing goes, the Daleks are pretty dangerous creatures, but surely if you were intent on any kind of significant destruction, let alone planetary takeover, you'd send more than four of your mates to get the job done?

It could be argued that the potential of other monsters from season nine wasn't fully realized either. Next up was the "ferocious" Aggedor from the planet Peladon. With Aggedor's fearsome roar, the viewer was probably expecting a little more than a five-foot-something bloke dressed in a furry costume. The Sea Devils had immobile heads on top of improbably long necks, just to ensure the actor could see—like an alien reptile version of a pantomime horse.

Sadly, however, the designers excelled themselves with the dreadful Gellguards, shapeless blobs of jelly that sounded like Mr. Bean and who featured in "The Three Doctors"—a tale that opened the tenth anniversary year of the series and brought together all the Doctor's three incarnations to battle a renegade Time Lord named Omega.

William Hartnell was not a well man, however, and he had to read his lines from a cue card whilst sitting in a chair—his pre-filmed image appeared on a screen inside the TARDIS. This would be Hartnell's last acting performance, and he passed away just under two and a half years later, on April 24, 1975.

Jo's final adventure was "The Green Death," set in Wales and featuring giant maggots and dead bodies that glowed bright gre... you're one step ahead again aren't you?! It was there that Jo met and fell in love with Professor Clifford Jones (Stewart Bevan). She agreed to marry Jones, and that decision brought an end to her travels with the Doctor.

Katy Manning

There was a particularly moving scene at a party for the newly engaged couple. The Doctor and Jo talked briefly and embraced before Jo rejoined her fiancé—the Doctor slipped out unnoticed and drove away, very much alone.

It was a moment of realization for the audience. The Doctor was simply a wanderer and ultimately, for all his knowledge and abilities, he had no power to control the feelings of his companions. In that single moment, the Doctor was seen for what he actually was: the "odd one out." It was a farewell scene of genuine emotion.

Somewhat bizarrely, I received two lots of photos from Katy Manning, a couple of days apart in January 2011. The second, which follows, is from the slightly easier to read batch. I do admire Katy's persistence, and her obvious desire to feature heavily in the book has, I hope, been rewarded.

Catherine Anne Manning was born in Surrey in October 1946; her father James was a noted sports journalist, who married Amy Sylvia Jenkins in her native Wales in 1939.

Katy has acted, written, and directed during her long and varied career. But for a couple of years in the early 1970s she was Jo Grant—petite, pretty, with the cutest of giggles (watch "The Green Death" if you don't believe me)—and had we been of more comparable ages, I reckon I would have had a massive crush on her!

Katy Manning

ANOTHER ROLL OF THE DICE

During the 1970s—particularly, it has to be said, during the Tom Baker era—many of the *Doctor Who* stories were given generic titles using one of several words designed to indicate impending disaster: "evil," "doom," "fear," "death," etc.

All you had to do was start with "the," select your second word, "planet," "robots," "city," "face," etc., add "of", and then roll the *Doctor-Who*-story-creating dice to complete the process.

"The Planet of Evil," "The City of Death," "The Seeds of Doom."

And the sadly discarded tale about a curry-eating monster: "The Rear of . . . Fear."

Right at the start of the decade, on March 21, 1970, to be exact, our television screen actually showed this very process in action, as the full title was initially only half revealed. Cue music: "The Ambassadors. . . ."

Is that all? Well that's a strange title for a *Doctor Who* story. Hang on, they must be rolling the dice. Maybe it's "The Ambassadors of Evil"? "Doom" perhaps? No, I know, it's "The Ambassadors of Fear."

But then the second half of the title was unveiled. Ahh . . . "The Ambassadors of Death"! Well that was all very dramatic.

This seven-part adventure was the third of the four stories that made up series seven. It was therefore Caroline John's third, yet penultimate, appearance as Liz Shaw.

The tale involves three missing astronauts from Mars Probe 7 and three aliens—whose identity is hidden by their spacesuits—who appear in their place. At the start of the opening episode, a recovery mission is underway, coordinated by Ralph Cornish (played by Ronald Allen, or David Hunter from *Crossroads* if you prefer).

Alien signals are heard and triangulated to an abandoned warehouse—which isn't actually abandoned—and it seems that the astronauts have been recovered from Mars Probe 7 but are being held in quarantine due to dangerously high radiation levels.

There is clearly something afoot as the Doctor and Brigadier's attempts at getting information and assistance are consistently flat-batted by government minister Sir James Quinlan and the military's General Carrington.

Scientist Dr. Bruno Tartalian is revealed to be working for both sides, and Reegan is introduced as the "villain," intent on making money out of what is evidently the presence of three aliens. Each alien has the ability—some might say gift—of being able to destroy on touch.

However, Quinlan is killed by one of the "astronauts," and Reegan does every viewer a huge favor by disposing of Tartalian's French accent and beard—it was tough to decide which was the more fake of the two.

The Doctor realizes that the real astronauts must still be in orbit, and despite Reegan's exhaustive attempts at sabotage, he flies into space and ends up on the alien craft, where he finds the missing astronauts and learns that the three creatures back on Earth are actually ambassadors of their race.

Back on terra firma, the Doctor rustles up a translation device, which confirms the ambassadors are peaceful and can't understand why they are being made to kill... and General Carrington is unmasked as the man behind the operation—not that the Doctor was remotely surprised.

Carrington was a former astronaut who had seen his fellow crew mates killed by members of this alien species, and he is intent on telling the world about an imminent extra-terrestrial invasion. All's well that ends well though, as Carrington is arrested and the ambassadors are finally able to return home—in exchange for the Mars Probe 7 crew.

Before I offer my opinion as to whether or not this story works, there are several moments that need to be mentioned, for better or for worse.

First of all, there is the huge amount of padding that allows the story to fill seven episodes. While I accept that a number of different writers were involved, and continuity was an issue at times, some of the scenes are ludicrously long and add little to the plot or the drama: The shots of satellite dishes, several protracted scenes involving UNIT troops, the chases (by car and then on foot) featuring Liz, and the absurdly extended sabotage attempt by Reegan to name but a few. If the story was filmed now, it would probably be condensed nicely into an hour and a half or less.

The next irritation is Tartalian's accent—I'm ignoring the beard because the accent is even more annoying. During the late 1960s, *Doctor Who* seemed to enjoy using a host of Anglicized accents (viz. "The Tenth Planet," "The Moonbase," "The Tomb of the Cybermen," "The Enemy of the World," "The Wheel in Space"—although based on looks alone, I'm prepared to forgive Clare Jenkins as Tanya Lernov), the mastery of which was clearly beyond some of the actors concerned.

Robert Cawdron is one of the worst offenders though, because his French inflection, so evident during internal shots, disappears completely when filming ventures outside the studio. Listen when he says "Get in Miss Shaw" in episode four: every inch the perfect English gentleman.

Some of the incidental music was pretty awful too; the docking of the rescue craft with Mars Probe 7, whilst visually impressive, is ruined by something that sounds like the Hamlet cigar advert.

There are other questions that need to be answered too. Such as, how did Reegan gain entry so easily to a high-security installation when he was driving a bakery van?

"Baps for the Brigadier."

"Just go straight in, Sir!"

And why was an ambassador able to kill Quinlan and destroy a safe simply by touch, yet could initially close an office door with nothing happening?

However, there are some champagne moments too: The Brigadier leading his UNIT troops from the front, revolver in hand, just like Captain Mainwaring in the *Dad's Army* closing credits; and his "fight" during which a punch misses the Brigadier by a country mile, yet Lethbridge-Stewart still hits the floor as if poleaxed—a technique apparently copied (and in plenty of cases mastered) by many a professional footballer. That said, I really enjoyed Liz telling the Doctor: "Well that'll be the analogue digital converter." You go girl!

As for the story itself, well it seems to have split reviewers pretty much down the middle, but I feel that despite its obvious flaws, there is a lot to recommend "The Ambassadors of Death." For starters, the "monsters" are not the villains of the piece, despite the human response of taking first impressions at face (or helmet) value. Reegan is probably the nearest thing to a "baddie," although he is basically a criminal motivated by greed and ruthless enough to use a situation to his advantage.

As for General Carrington, it becomes clear that the loss of his crew, literally at the hands of the ambassadors, has tipped him over the edge. Outwardly composed and genuinely convinced he is right in his beliefs, Carrington is misguided to the point of irrational instability, although his position ultimately provokes sympathy—something which the Doctor recognizes, and the General is at least able to retain his dignity, if not his liberty.

So, therefore, we are faced with a tale of morality rather than the standard human versus alien battle for planetary supremacy.

We are left to ponder the fact that we immediately assume the worst about something we simply don't understand. The perceived threat of the creatures from another world is amply demonstrated by their ability to destroy—or is it?

Again, we make an assumption that is subsequently proven to be unfounded and, in truth, the only real danger to the population comes from ourselves and our fear of the unknown.

Another theme of some Earth-based adventures is the apparent treachery of high-ranking officials (viz. General Finch in "Invasion of the Dinosaurs"). If you can't trust those in charge then just who *can* you trust?

Add to that some excellent cliff hangers, and the suspense that can be created by gradual revelation, and you end up with a thought-provoking piece of television—not perfect, but absorbing and impressive for a drama transmitted over four decades ago.

Caroline John 1940-2012

LOOKING GOOD MA'AM

Sarah Jane Smith was the most enduring, and arguably the most popular, of all *Doctor Who* companions. The character's first adventure was in 1973, and her final appearance was alongside David Tennant in the two-part tale "The End of Time," over thirty-six years later. The second episode was aired on New Year's Day 2010 and marked Tennant's regeneration into Matt Smith's incarnation of the Time Lord.

Sarah Jane's appeal may, in part, stem from the fact that the series was enjoying a golden period in the mid-1970s. Both Jon Pertwee and Tom Baker were well-liked, and their respective reputations have remained intact despite the passing decades, but that is to take nothing away from Elisabeth Sladen's portrayal of the journalist turned time traveler.

It all started with Sarah Jane impersonating her aunt, the virologist Lavinia Smith, because she was hot on the trail of a scoop involving the disappearance of a number of eminent scientists. Her professional curiosity brought her into contact with the Doctor and also a squat alien named Linx—a Sontaran warrior with an extremely ugly face but curiously appealing underarm odor.

She then encountered some particularly unconvincing dinosaurs in London (as you do), before a story set on the planet Exxilon. "Death to the Daleks" featured a city that was draining energy, but which was almost "alive," and any attempt to enter was fraught with danger thanks to a series of potentially lethal traps. The Doctor faced a race not only against time, but also against a small force of Daleks who were in hot pursuit, to reach the center of the city and destroy its brain.

This was Sarah Jane's first visit to an alien world, and this atmospheric tale was one of the highlights of season eleven.

Unfortunately, Aggedor then reared his horned head as the TARDIS returned to Peladon. A poor story, but a chance for actor Nick Hobbs to update his CV: "I played a scary, yet strangely cuddly creature in *Doctor Who* ... twice."

Incidentally, this signed photo of Lis Sladen is a still from "The Monster of Peladon."

Elisabeth Sladen

The season drew to a close with a six-parter set on Earth and the planet Metebelis III, where the locals lived in fear of a race of giant spiders. Sarah Jane fell under the telepathic control of the "Eight Legs" and the Doctor was ultimately left with no option but to "face his fear" in the form of the Great One, the most powerful of all the spiders.

He entered the Great One's cave, where the increasing power from a crystal lattice sent her insane, the cave exploded, and all the spiders were killed.

Back on Earth, Sarah—now restored to her normal self—and members of UNIT waited for the Doctor's return. His body had been badly damaged by radiation and, right in front of disbelieving eyes, the Doctor's features began to blur and change.

As an aside (yes, another one), one of the spider voices was provided by Kismet Delgado, wife of Roger Delgado. Actually, that should read "widow," as the actor who portrayed the Master had been tragically killed in a car accident in June 1973, just under a year before "Planet of the Spiders" was transmitted.

And as an aside to the aside: Maureen Morris was another of those who voiced the spiders. You probably won't have heard of her, but if any die-hard *Coronation Street* fans can recall Maureen Barnett, who had a short stint behind the Rovers Return bar in 1985, then I can tell you that barmaid and spider voice were one and the same.

Sarah Jane's personality was further developed alongside Tom Baker's Doctor, and the pair were joined by Harry Sullivan (played by the late Ian Marter). Sarah was lacking little in confidence and inquisitiveness, and she revealed herself to be both strong-willed and capable of forming close bonds with her companions. Tom Baker's first season as the incumbent Time Lord also threw up an all-time classic: "Genesis of the Daleks."

The trio were transported to Skaro at a point in time when the brilliant—but glaringly obvious megalomaniac—Kaled scientist Davros was on the verge of creating the beings that would assume a name that was an anagram of his people.

The pivotal moment of a tense and sometimes genuinely scary story—and please bear in mind that I was only ten at the time—saw the Doctor wrestling with his conscience as he looked at two wires which, if touched together, would obliterate Davros's genetic experiments and destroy the Daleks forever.

The Doctor revealed his dilemma: "If someone who knew the future pointed out a child to you and told you that that child would grow up totally evil, to be a ruthless dictator who would destroy millions of lives; could you then kill that child?"

"We're talking about the Daleks; the most evil creatures ever invented. You must destroy them," replied Sarah.

I was with Sarah Jane on this one: *Touch the bloody wires together!!* Not that I used words like that when I was ten.

The moment passed and the opportunity was lost—just as we all knew it would be. But as a whole, it's an excellent story, and the characters of Davros and his "nasty piece of work" sidekick Nyder are superbly realized.

However, I haven't had an aside for all of . . . ooh . . . one page, but on opposing sides in this adventure were Guy Siner and Hilary Minster, who would later join forces as German army soldiers in the wartime sit-com *'Allo 'Allo.*

Season thirteen was a mix of the good, the bad, and the indifferent. Top of the pile is "Pyramids of Mars," in which an Egyptian God (Sutekh) manifested himself in a Victorian manor house complete with cloth-wrapped robotic dummies.

The festivities culminated on Mars with a series of logic problems (reminiscent of "Death to the Daleks"), success in the last of which was vital to save the life of Sarah Jane, who had been trapped inside a transparent cylinder and—cue dramatic music—with the air supply diminishing, she would soon suffocate.

The Doctor was faced with a simple but stark choice between two switches. Choosing the right one would save his friend but the outcome wouldn't be quite so good if he picked the "death switch." Two mummified robots (the Guardians of Horus) held the proverbial key.

They were contra-programmed so that one would always tell the truth while the other was a compulsive liar. The Doctor was permitted one question to one of the Guardians to solve the conundrum.

His question was: If the other Guardian was asked to point to the "life switch," which would he indicate?

The premise was that the truth Guardian would point to the death switch because that's what his lying counterpart would say. Likewise, the false Guardian would also indicate the death switch in a bid to deceive. Therefore, whichever Guardian the Doctor chose, both would raise their arm towards the death switch. So all the Doctor had to do was press the other button and Sarah would be freed.

I remember being amazed by this riddle at the time, even though I wasn't sure if the logic stacked up. I'm older and wiser now and realize it was just quality padding—tense and clever, yes—but padding nonetheless.

Sarah Jane bowed out of the regular series in October 1976, in a story entitled "The Hand of Fear," but reprised her role in a 1981 spin-off, *K-9 and Company*, with the robotic dog that had first featured in *Doctor Who* four years earlier.

Then, nearly a quarter of a century later, Sarah and the Doctor were reunited at Deffry Vale School, where something sinister was afoot.

The character of Sarah Jane Smith subsequently appeared in several more stories, as well as a series of her own, *The Sarah Jane Adventures*—not a great deal of thought went into that title methinks! Here is a signed publicity shot from that series.

There is little, or no, doubt that of all the companions to have crossed the TARDIS threshold, Sarah Jane Smith made the biggest—and definitely the longest lasting—contribution to the ongoing popularity of the show;

Elisabeth Sladen

the character transcended the generations, and it was a terrible shock to hear the news of Elisabeth Sladen's passing on April 19, 2011.

She had been battling cancer, but it appears that only her closest relatives were aware of the illness. The next chapter, by way of a tribute to Lis Sladen, is a review of "The Ark in Space," a story that featured both Sarah Jane and Harry Sullivan alongside Tom Baker's Doctor. Stories from that era can occasionally whisk you briefly back to a time of your life that was filled with innocence instead of responsibility, and I just find it incredibly sad to think that Lis Sladen, Ian Marter, and also Nicholas Courtney (who played the Brigadier) are all no longer with us—Courtney having died just two months before Lis's untimely passing.

COMMITTING INSECTICIDE

The "Ark in Space" was Tom Baker's second story. On the surface, it appears to be another "Doctor arrives just in time to battle and defeat an alien threat" tale, but actually it's a whole lot better than that. (This may be evidenced by revived series producers Russell T. Davies and Steven Moffat both claiming this as their favorite story from the show's original run.)

To understand why, you certainly need to look beyond the extra-terrestrial adversary: the Wirrn, scuttling insect-like creatures that are nothing better than reasonably convincing.

Worse, though, is the unashamed use of green bubble wrap to create the effect of human skin mutating into Wirrn, and as for the caterpillar—shhh... it's a green sleeping bag—shuffling around Nerva Beacon, sorry it just doesn't quite work for me.

But although some stages of the Wirrn's development look like they were cobbled together on *Blue Peter*, the story does possess claustrophobic tension and several scary moments for the younger audience.

If the designers ultimately failed with aspects of the Wirrn, they excelled themselves with the story's setting, Nerva Beacon: curved corridors (plural, although the reality was probably singular), believable control rooms, a cryogenic chamber, and a particularly nasty, but nicely-conceived, autoguard.

The first episode is unusual—albeit excellently so—in that it essentially features just the three TARDIS crew members: the Doctor, Sarah Jane, and Harry Sullivan. To find a similar occurrence you would have to go back eleven years to the two-part William Hartnell tale "The Edge of Destruction" (or "Inside the Spaceship" if you prefer). That story was a vehicle to introduce the viewers to the new characters, and in a sense the opening twenty-odd minutes of "The Ark in Space" does the same. Harry and the newly-regenerated Time Lord both get some good lines and decent interaction, as the more established Sarah is separated from her companions and transported into the cryogenic chamber.

Harry's outwardly straight-laced, old-school manner does not manage to hide an ironic sense of humor, made all the better by Ian Marter's deadpan delivery: "I'm trying to remember. It's awfully difficult, I can hardly breathe."

The scenes with the autoguard also work well, although Harry's girlie throw of the cricket ball suggests he's not quite as proficient in the game as he may have believed.

We have already been given a couple of teasers regarding the alien menace that was lying in wait—including a human called Dune in a state of suspended animation, seen through a jellified eye.

The next scene was actually removed from the final cut, but featured two Wirrn parodying Laurel and Hardy: "His name is Dune and very, very soon, he'll belong to me. For I know he's waiting there for me, 'neath that lone ... er ... cryogenic casket."

The design of the chamber bears comparison with the Cybermen's "tomb" from the 1967 story, but in theory this is on an altogether grander scale given the fact that the Beacon is supposed to be housing the whole of the human race. Clever use of camera angles gives the chamber more of a sense of scale, and even though we only see a handful of the crew woken from their slumber, I think the concept of the cryogenic store works.

As for the Wirrn; well the adult costume is slightly more believable than that of the larvae, but perhaps it's fair to say that more money was spent on the scenery than the enemy. What struck me immediately was the resemblance between the fully grown insect-like Wirrn and the Martian creatures that featured in *Quatermass and the Pit*—the brilliant Hammer version of which had reached the big screen less than a decade earlier.

There are further echoes of the movie with the use of the term "race memory" followed by the Doctor's mind being used to project images originally seen through the eyes of the Wiirn Queen. In the film, Barbara Judd (played by Hammer favorite Barbara Shelley) is the person capable of seeing long-suppressed memories, and these similarities are strong enough to indicate that the writers (Robert Holmes and the uncredited John Lucarotti) may have been influenced to some degree by the Quatermass genre.

And in case you're interested, Barbara Shelley played Sorasta in the 1984 Peter Davison story, "Planet of Fire."

In fact, she played Sorasta even if you're not interested.

Having mentioned the alien Queen, I was going to add an amusing little comment about the part being offered to the renowned Queen-playing actress Helen Wirrn, but luckily I decided against it.

Of the human characters, well it doesn't take Noah long to come into contact with some green slime and start turning into bubble wrap. How obvious is it that there is something very wrong with Noah's left hand as he minces around with it firmly planted in his trouser pocket?

The truth is soon revealed, amid much overacting.

Noah's designated love interest, Vira, is first to be roused, but she can only stand and watch helplessly as Noah's hand, then arm and face turn into "go on have a pop if you're hard enough" green-tinted stress relief. Libri gets blasted to death, simply because Christopher Masters's acting was so bad, and Lycett meets his fate and the hands—or rather the antennae—of the Wirrn. Rogin dies in an act of quite touching self-sacrifice, and the transformed Noah retains just enough of his former mind to destroy himself—and the Wirrn swarm—after a final intercom farewell to his intended.

I drew a parallel here with the Tracy-Anne Oberman Cyberman in "Doomsday"—all in all, the last vestige of humanity card is a great one to play when there looks to be no way out.

Having watched the four parts again, I am not sure that the conclusion lives up to the intriguing opening episode, but ultimately this is a story that includes both good and indifferent effects, a cast portraying human characters of varying believability, and some moments of genuine claustrophobic suspense.

Bubble wrap aside, "The Ark in Space" probably stands the test of time and, fittingly, pride of place for me goes to Sarah Jane Smith. Onscreen, her character was still coming to terms with a regenerated Doctor, but Elisabeth Sladen was by far the most established of the main actors and her performance shines like a (Nerva) beacon.

Baker and Sladen were about to embark on one of *Doctor Who*'s most popular partnerships, and the scene where Sarah is cajoled to the point of being ridiculed and bullied when "trapped" in a narrow ventilation shaft is a wonderful foretaste of things to come.

And a moving reminder of someone taken far too soon.

Elisabeth Sladen 1946-2011

DEAF TO THE DALEKS

Unusually for *Doctor Who*, there was a brief hiatus between companions after Sarah Jane's departure. The gap was filled with a dramatic story set on Gallifrey, where the Doctor was accused of assassinating the outgoing Time Lord President.

The Doctor was framed as part of an elaborate plot by a dying Master to gain control of the Presidency and the traditional symbols of office, which were in reality keys to the Eye of Harmony, the source of all the Time Lords' power. I wasn't yet a teenager and I remember "The Deadly Assassin" as being one of the most terrifying adventures I'd ever seen.

The Doctor's new assistant, Leela, was revealed (almost completely) in a story entitled "The Face of Evil," the first installment of which was aired on New Year's Day 1977. The plot featured a race of barbarians called the Sevateem, a corrupted name that indicated their origins as a spaceship survey team. Leela was a scantily-clad, fearless warrior who, much to the Doctor's displeasure, thought nothing of killing an adversary with a knife or paralysis-inducing Janis thorn.

Series producer Chris Boucher envisaged that Leela would be a mix of the dynamic Emma Peel from *The Avengers* and, somewhat bizarrely, a Palestinian terrorist named Leila Khaled, whose name Boucher "borrowed" for the new character.

Despite her primitive appearance, Leela was intelligent and astute enough to be able to grasp advanced ideas and translate them into concepts with which she was more familiar.

Actually that should come with the caveat of "usually", because in "The Robots of..."—roll those dice—"Death," Leela believed that the TARDIS would only keep flying providing the Doctor's yo-yo was spinning.

"The Robots of Death" was one of two really strong stories in which Leela featured; the other was the subsequent adventure that brought season fourteen to a close, "The Talons of Weng-Chiang"—no dice required for that one. The respective settings created bags of suspense and atmosphere: namely a futuristic mining craft and the mist of Victorian London.

Louise Jameson

On board the Sandminer, the crew was being systematically dispatched one-by-one by server robots who had been reprogrammed by a brilliant, but misguided, scientist named Taren Capel, who was masquerading as chief engineer Dask.

Capel was defeated when Leela released helium into the air so that the killer robots no longer recognized—nor obeyed—Capel's voice.

"The Talons of Weng-Chiang" was your average run-of-the-mill tale of disappearing women, a mysterious Chinese magician, a ventriloquist's dummy—that genuinely had a life of its own—a giant rat, and a renegade criminal from the fifty-first century. The rat may not have been particularly realistic—mainly because it was a model—but at least Louise Jameson was given the chance to enjoy a costume change, as the murky Victorian London streets were no place for a partially dressed savage. She might have looked demure but don't be fooled, she was still a dangerous woman.

By contrast, season fifteen was far less memorable. The series opener "The Horror of Fang Rock" was set in a lighthouse and showcased the Rutans (sworn enemies of the Sontarans), whose natural form resembled a space hopper. "The Invisible Enemy" followed—a cracking idea when you're looking to save money, but a dreadful story.

The final story, "The Invasion of Time," was set on Gallifrey, but unlike Sarah Jane, Leela was allowed to visit the Doctor's home planet. The adventure marked a return for the battle-hungry Sontarans, who were still suffering from "small man syndrome," and an exit for Leela who somehow found the time to fall in love with a chap called Andred and decided to remain on Gallifrey—a rather unbelievable end to a poor season.

On the plus side, the two photos of Louise Jameson that are reproduced in this chapter were received in September 2012, and are therefore appearing in *Desperately Seeking Susan Foreman* for the first time. Louise was born in April 1951, and in addition to her time in *Doctor Who*, she has appeared in television series such as *Emmerdale Farm* (as it was called in 1973 when she played Sharon Crossthwaite), *Tenko*, *Bergerac*, *Eastenders*, and *Doc Martin*.

But some thirty-something years after she left the TARDIS, Louise Jameson is arguably still most associated with Leela and *Doctor Who*, and this quote from a 2008 interview may partially explain why:

> I think the BBC said: 'We'll have this feisty, intelligent, interesting woman, but we'll take her clothes off for an outfit!' I thought I was going to be in a kids' TV series, I had absolutely no idea that she'd be in those clothes and she'd end up a sex-symbol.
>
> With the wisdom of hindsight, of course, put someone in a leather leotard after the football results, and inevitably you're going to get a load of the male population tuning in!

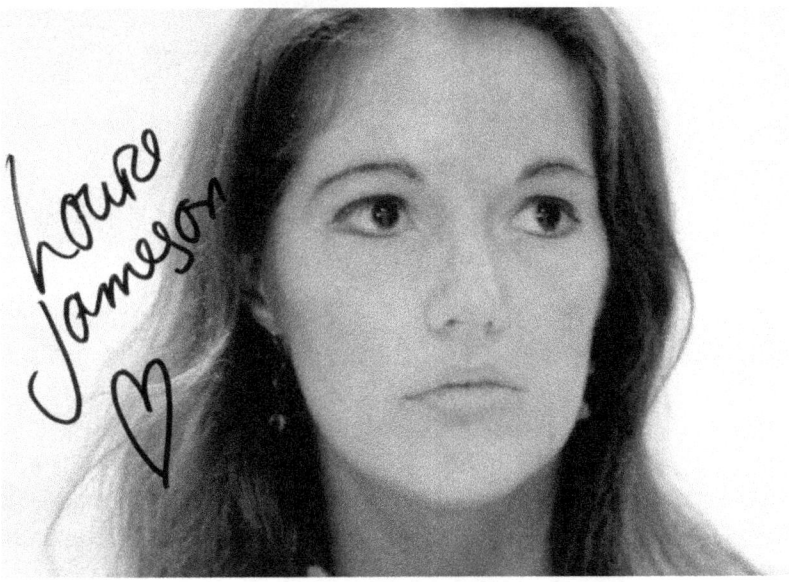

Louise Jameson

The conceptual season sixteen introduced Mary Tamm as Romana (I'm not going to try and spell her full name) along with the White and Black Guardians—equal and opposing forces above the Time Lords who held the very balance of the universe in their supremely powerful hands.

Although the Doctor had been paired with a couple of highly intelligent companions (in Zoë and Liz), the character of Romana went one stage further. Not only was she from Gallifrey but she was also every bit as clever as her fellow Time Lord and this, added to the fact that Mary Tamm brought undeniable glamour to the role, set apart the first incarnation of Romana from almost every other companion.

Mary herself was already an established actress, but her accent—perfected at RADA during the late 1960s—disguised the fact that she was actually born in Yorkshire, to Estonian parents. Apparently, Tamm is a relatively common surname in Estonia and means "oak" or "oak tree."

The signed photo that follows was actually the very first one I received when the original quest got underway back early in 2010.

Mary Tamm

Anyway, the season's underlying theme was to collect the six segments of the cube-shaped Key to Time—which was the source of the Guardians' power—and to reassemble the pieces to preserve the stability of the cosmos.

Very cleverly, the season comprised six separate stories, thereby allowing each segment to be given its own adventure. Now I don't want to spoil things for anyone who has bought the DVD box set and has not yet got round to watching it . . . but I'm going to.

The first segment was a lump of the rare element Jethryk on the planet Ribos, the second was the miniaturized planet Callufrax, segment three was the Great Seal of Diplos, four was part of a statue on the planet Tara, the fifth was swallowed by a giant squid-like creature Kroll, and finally, the all-important sixth piece was none other than Lalla Ward herself in the guise of Princess Astra of Atrios.

With the cube now fully assembled, the White Guardian appeared on the TARDIS scanner and asked for the Key to be released to him. The Doctor enquired what would happen to Astra if the segments remained intact, as permanent imprisonment within the cube would essentially mean she no longer existed. The White Guardian explained that the situation was "regrettable," but the interests of the universe had to come first.

The Doctor feigned agreement then quickly engaged the TARDIS's defenses, having realized that the White Guardian's attitude to life would never have been so callous and that the Black Guardian was actually masquerading as his White counterpart.

His true identity uncovered, an enraged Black Guardian swore vengeance on the Doctor, but our hero had set up a randomizer in the TARDIS on the basis that if he didn't have a clue where he was going to land next, the Black Guardian didn't have much hope of finding him.

The Doctor finally dispersed the six parts of the Key around the universe, an action that duly brought back Astra, and all was well once again.

Believing the character of Romana had developed as far as it could, Mary Tamm elected not to return for a second season, and that decision paved the way for a regeneration and a new Romana: Lalla Ward.

Lalla was born in June 1951; her actual name is Sarah, and as the daughter of Edward, Viscount Bangor, she is entitled to use the title the Honorable Sarah Ward. She apparently acquired the nickname Lalla from her early attempts at pronouncing her real name.

On taking the role of Romana and her recollections of the series, Lalla once revealed in a BBC interview:

I played Princess whatever her name was, Astra. Mary [Tamm] wasn't sure whether she was going to do it or not and I sort of drifted into it I think because Tom [Baker] got on so well with me and it was easy. So in a way, there weren't really any early memories, it just happened.

As for watching it, I never really did as a child because we didn't watch all that much television. [but] I said, 'Oh yes, I hid behind the sofa like everybody else,' you know!

Aside from acting, Lalla (who married the evolutionary biologist Richard Dawkins in 1992) is a noted book illustrator and skilled embroiderer. She has also served on the committee of The Actors' Charitable Trust for over two decades.

Anyway, the second incarnation of Romana was much more of a free spirit than her predecessor; in fact, the second Romana was in many ways a female version of the Doctor—even copying his outfit in the opening scenes of "Destiny of the Daleks."

Lalla Ward

I remember enjoying that particular story at the time. It was set on Skaro and featured the Daleks (fairly obviously), who were involved in a struggle against a race called the Movellans—who turned out to be androids. The two sides had been locked in a stalemate that had lasted centuries, and the Daleks were attempting to find their creator Davros, who had been buried underground as a consequence of the explosion that concluded "Genesis of the Daleks."

Ultimately, the Movellans end up deactivated, the Daleks are defeated, and Davros is captured; all in all a good day's work for the Time Lord and his Gallifreyan sidekick.

The four episodes are still watchable, but some of the effects are either dated or, in the case of an immovable concrete column, very poor, as the polystyrene shifted every time it was touched. Worse still, the way Davros lurched around the underground bunker was straight out of the duck manual—visibly calm, but legs flapping away like mad below the surface.

From the point of view of the main characters, Baker and Ward seemed to work well together and we all know where the onscreen chemistry led! As for the supporting cast, there were one or two interesting names.

Of the Movellans: Lan was played by Tony Osoba, the Scottish-born actor best known for his role as Jock McLaren in *Porridge*; and Agella was played by the gorgeous Suzanne Danielle, whose partner at the time (Patrick Mower) was a regular on set, keeping a beady eye on his ambitious young girlfriend (according to the DVD commentary).

Tim Barlow, who played the escaped captive Tyssan, was profoundly deaf—not that you could tell—having lost his hearing whilst in the Army during the 1950s. Tim had a cochlear implant fitted in 2008, allowing him to hear for the first time in half a century.

I mention this because in 1996, I lost the hearing in my right ear as a result of a sudden viral attack that pretty much destroyed my cochlea (the swirly bit in the inner ear). If I deliberately sit to your left, you'll now understand why....

Anyway, season seventeen included the story that achieved the highest ever ratings for any *Doctor Who* adventure, as episode three of "City of Death" attracted over sixteen million viewers.

It should be noted that ITV was not broadcasting at the time, due to a strike, so the feat is not as noteworthy as it first appears. That said, the circumstances were hardly the fault of the BBC, and the escapade was arguably good enough to warrant a sizeable audience.

The Doctor and Romana were enjoying a holiday in contemporary Paris when they became aware of a fracture in time. You look forward all year to your break and then something like that happens!

Anyway, the Doctor pinched a bracelet from a stranger (Countess Scarlioni) that turned out to be an alien scanning device, and at the palatial home of the Count, they found six paintings of the Mona Lisa—all originals.

The Count was revealed as a bloke in a silly mask —sorry, as an alien named Scaroth, last of the Jagaroth race—and he was intent on traveling back in time to prevent his spaceship from being destroyed. The ensuing explosion had caused Scaroth's being to be splintered across various eras but in actual fact also brought about the creation of life on Earth—you read it here first—and the Doctor was forced to follow Scaroth back to primeval times to ensure the proper course of history.

Scarlioni/Scaroth was played by Julian Glover, who had appeared as Richard the Lionheart in the William Hartnell story "The Crusade." Glover also took the role of Colonel Breen in *Quatermass and the Pit*, the 1967 movie mentioned during "The Ark in Space" review.

Breen was the aloof intransigent military nemesis of Professor Quatermass, stubbornly insisting that despite glaring evidence to the contrary, every object and event witnessed at the Hobbs End underground dig could be explained away as German World War II propaganda—a misguided theory that ultimately cost Breen his life as the Martian purge gathered momentum.

There was little of note in the next story, "Creature from the Pit," except perhaps the reappearance of Eileen Way—who had featured in the first ever *Doctor Who* adventure—and one of those "I recognize that face from somewhere" moments in the form of Geoffrey Bayldon—best known as the eccentric wizard *Catweazle* from the children's television series of the same name.

The "Horns of Nimon" introduced a bloke-in-a-costume monster with a "fearsome" horned head. Hang on . . . that's just like Aggedor.

Well, Nick Hobbs must have been chomping at the proverbial bit come audition time: "Horned aliens? Well I'm your man!"

Incredibly, of the three actors who were eventually cast to play one of these Nimon creatures, precisely none were called Nick Hobbs. A disconsolate Hobbs could only reflect that Aggedor had just the one horn: the

Nimons had two, and in terms of required acting ability, the transition was evidently too great.

The season ended farcically with the Douglas Adams penned "Shada" not making it onto our screens, as studio time to complete recording ran out due to a backlog of Christmas specials. Formally dropped in 1979, efforts were made to finish the story but to no avail, and whilst Tom Baker provided linking for missing scenes to enable a video release in 1992, "Shada" has never been aired on television.

For the record, Shada was a lost planet on which the Time Lords had constructed a prison for those who had tried to conquer the universe—and failed.

New producer John Nathan-Turner oversaw a number of significant changes, not least of which was that Tom Baker's contract would not be extended and he would therefore leave the series at the conclusion of series eighteen. Baker's portrayal of the Time Lord had developed throughout his tenure, but Nathan-Turner was seemingly unimpressed with the flippancy that had been allowed to creep into the role.

The second story of season eighteen ("Meglos") was notable for the return of former companion Jacqueline Hill as Lexa and for the appearance of some sort of power-hungry cactus.

Three stories were then combined to form the "E-Space Trilogy," and at the end of the third of those adventures, "Warrior's Gate," Romana decided to remain (along with K-9) to help the native Tharils free their people, but not before a nasty moment at the end of episode two . . .

Romana was strapped to a chair, as a Tharil approached and reached for her face. Romana wasn't overly happy about the situation—in fact her scream of terror was strangely reminiscent of how I react to a check-up at the dentist.

Not that I'm suggesting my dentist has hairy hands, but it is fair to say that I don't find the whole experience particularly relaxing.

Having said that, you've got lovely teeth Romana. See you in six months.

62

THE COLOR PURPLE

In tribute to Mary Tamm's memory, here is a look back at the four-part story, "The Androids of Tara," which was broadcast during November and December 1978 (the first episode aired just two days after the series' fifteenth anniversary).

The previous chapter has given away the fact that the whole of season sixteen was built around the acquisition of the six segments of the Key to Time and that the fourth piece was located on the planet Tara—more specifically as part of a statue.

Luckily—or perhaps cleverly—Tara had an Earth-type gravity, oxygen, atmosphere, climate, and temperature, thus saving a fortune in set design. The comparison with Earth's flora and fauna was one thing, but somewhat bizarrely, the Taran marriage ceremony seen during the story was also more than just a little reminiscent of how we do things.

That apart, the TARDIS arrives on Ea . . . sorry, Tara, and much as Romana—dressed in an outfit that could best be described as purple—wants to get on with finding the fourth segment, the Doctor is equally keen to go fishing: "You find it; I'm taking the day off."

So, as the Doctor casts off, Romana locates the next piece of the Key to Time almost immediately. Easy peasy . . . next story.

But an "oh dear" moment soon follows with the intervention of the worst furry monster costume of all time. I take back everything I said about Aggedor and apologize unreservedly to Peladon's finest. Romana was duly rescued—although "captured" may be a better word—by Count Grendel of Gracht (baddie), whilst the Doctor encountered soldiers loyal to Prince Reynart (goodie).

Romana was taken to Gracht Castle, which looked reasonably impressive from a distance, although I understand that Leeds Castle (in Kent) and CSO were used to create the illusion of the building's exterior. As for Count Grendel: if the face looked vaguely familiar, actor Peter Jeffrey played the Pilot in the Patrick Troughton story "The Macra Terror."

The Doctor was duly acquainted with Reynart and was invited to mend an android facsimile of the Prince—the Doctor's quip about the "local android dealer" being the best person to ask not only fell on deaf ears but was also indicative of the comic asides heard throughout the story.

So, the basic premise of the adventure was that Reynart was due to be crowned King, Grendel was determined to go to any lengths to ensure this didn't happen as he had designs on the Taran throne, and the situation was complicated by the existence of Princess Strella—albeit as a prisoner of Grendel—who bore more than an uncanny resemblance to Romana.

With Mary Tamm playing the two roles—as well as android versions of both Romana and Strella—this meant that Mary Tamm was very much at the forefront of the story. She looks stunningly beautiful, and listening to her silky voice, no one would have guessed that English was not her family's native tongue.

The ability to use android doubles was essential to the plot, and if the viewer was ever confused as to which characters were real and which were the robot copies, the best way of spotting the difference was that the androids acted better.

Anyway, the old-fashioned nature of Tara—costumes, castles etc., and the fact that distances were measured in "leagues"—contrasted with crossbows that fired electronic bolts—albeit not very accurately on occasions.

If you watch Romana's escape on a horse, she passes a guard who contrives to fire the worst shot ever with an electric crossbow, missing the proverbial barn door by the equally proverbial country mile. But a little later, when Grendel's android maker Madam Lamia steps into range, she is inadvertently zapped with unerring accuracy by a guard who might be a better shot than his helmeted colleague but who is blatantly not very bright.

As the story reaches its climax, an unnecessarily long sword-fight takes place between Grendel and the Doctor. The baddies get their comeuppance—just as we knew they would—and Reynart and Strella presumably live happily ever after as Doctor bemoans the fact he hadn't caught one fish.

Should this story be taken as one part of a greater whole or can it be viewed in isolation? Probably both to a certain extent, but if I saw the other five adventures at the time I certainly can't remember, so I am going to simply look at "The Androids of Tara" as a standalone story.

Despite the misgivings about the setting—and I fully accept the budgetary constraints—I think the internal and external scenes look quite good and work reasonably well. Whether or not they convince the viewer that Tara is an alien planet—possible Earth colony or otherwise—is another question altogether though.

The androids referred to in the title of the story are little more than a means to an end: and that "end" is to create doubles of three main characters—even though two of them are identical. Money saved no doubt, but when one actress ends up playing four separate parts, some younger viewers would surely have become confused as the story unfolded.

The idea of having the central part of the story (the segment of the Key to Time) being uncovered in the opening moments of the first episode is a nice touch, but it is Peter Jeffrey who manages to keep the story afloat—his performance being the only one of note amongst the main Taran protagonists.

There is little that is memorable about the other characters, although it is interesting (albeit relatively) that Madam Lamia is the only person to be killed in the story—and that was by "friendly fire." This must have come as a relief to actor Cyril Shaps who was making the final of his four appearances in *Doctor Who* (he played the ridiculously named and equally ridiculously attired Archimandrite). Shaps had previously been seen as Viner in "The Tomb of the Cybermen," Lennox in "The Ambassadors of Death," and Clegg in "Planet of the Spiders," and none of these three characters lived to tell the tale, so at least he ended his *Doctor Who* career with a survival!

There seems to be quite a lot of (presumably scripted) humor injected into the piece by Tom Baker. I don't think that it saves what is undoubtedly an essentially dull story; in fact I believe there was a very definite move away from the comedic aspects of the Doctor's character as the season—and Baker's tenure—progressed.

In conclusion, "The Androids of Tara" is not a particularly strong story on its own, and I will leave it to others to consider its position within the theme of the series as a whole. There is a certain amount of promise in the plot, but the story, as with most of the characters, ultimately lacks any real depth and is largely forgettable as a result.

That said, it's not very often that one person gets to play four roles in one *Doctor Who* story and although opinion may be divided as to whether or not this was Mary Tamm's finest hour as the original incarnation of Romana, surely none of her fans would have objected to the extra screen time she received, and the chapter closes with one final picture of Mary, resplendent in a hat of unknown style, but it was very definitely purple.

Mary Tamm 1950-2012

ALL MONSTERS GREAT AND SMALL

Before this chapter gets properly underway, I think it's fair to say it won't exactly be brimming with signed photographs, so if you've acquired the book more for the pictures than the text, you need to start flicking the pages around about now.

For the rest of you, it's not too long until the Doctor Mark IV pays his visit to Regeneration City—two stories to be precise: "The Keeper of Traken" and "Logopolis." The former saw the introduction of Nyssa (played by the teenage actress Sarah Sutton), who joined the Doctor and Adric after the Master had consumed the body of her father Tremas in order to gain a new physical, human form—before dematerializing in his TARDIS, which had been disguised as a grandfather clock.

Nyssa was swiftly followed by Tegan Jovanka (Janet Fielding), a feisty Australian air hostess who, along with her two fellow traveling companions, watched as the fourth incarnation of the Doctor transformed into... Tristan Farnon?

It shouldn't happen to a Time Lord.

Peter Davison (born Peter Moffett) was still in his twenties when he was cast as the fifth Doctor and remained the youngest to have taken on the role until Matt Smith (who was twenty-six). At this point, I will have to admit to seeing very few of Davison's stories—the same applies to Messrs Baker (Colin) and McCoy—but my research will be thorough (well, it might be).

So anyway, the TARDIS and its crew dematerialized from Darrowby, landed on the planet Castrovalva, and straight into a trap laid by the Master.

The season's third story was entitled "Kinda"—a bit of a surprise—and saw Tegan fall under the power of the evil Mara. The Mara existed in the minds of its victims and survived on their fear; it could also manifest itself as a giant snake—all in all, not very nice then.

The adventure was set on Deva Loka, a planet made famous by the Ricky Martin song, but more notable was the long overdue return of the Cybermen in a story called "Earthshock." John Nathan-Turner had actively wanted to engineer the reappearance of some of the series' most enduring and popular monsters—the Daleks would also battle with Davison's Doctor.

Anyway, the Cybermen were planning to detonate a bomb and destroy an upcoming peace conference; they had an army hidden in an approaching freighter.

In an attempt to foil the Cybermen, Adric somehow sent the freighter millions of years back in time, where it caused the explosion that brought about the extinction of the dinosaurs.

Back inside the TARDIS, Tegan and Nyssa were in tears and the Doctor watched on impassively as Adric lost his life in the blast, before the end credits rolled in silence.

At the time, *Doctor Who* was being transmitted twice weekly, and so keen were producers to keep the identity of the Doctor's foe a secret that the Cyberleader was listed simply as "Leader" in the *Radio Times*.

The season closed with "Time-Flight," another story featuring the Master—this one involving a trip on Concorde, right back to prehistoric times. The Master had been portrayed by actor Anthony Ainley since the tragic death of Roger Delgado (apart from Peter Pratt's role in "The Deadly Assassin"), and in both this tale and "Castrovalva," the Master had appeared as other characters, with the letters of Tony Ainley being rearranged into a fictitious name in the end credits in a bid to confuse viewers.

In "Castrovalva," Ainley played the Portreeve and was credited as Neil Toynay, which seems plausible enough, but the part of Kalid in "Time-Flight" was apparently played by Leon Ny Taiy.

Sorry, who? Surely that's almost as big a giveaway as actually putting his real name!

However, I do have three suggestions of my own: Lenny Iota (he came from a Greek family), Noel Yintay, or what about Joe's father—Ayol Ninety?

Anyhow, as far as the respective personalities of the two girls was concerned, Nyssa was selfless and unassuming, whereas Tegan was stubborn, loud, and very much "in your face." Tegan also had a major weakness as far as the Mara was concerned, as it regained control of her once again in a story called "Snakedance," which also marked the television debut of Martin Clunes.

The subsequent three stories in season twenty reintroduced the Black and White Guardians and were known collectively as "The Guardian Trilogy"—someone will have been paid good money to think that up.

John Nathan-Turner had decided the time was right for Nyssa to be written out of the series. He had actually wanted to replace her during the previous season but Peter Davison felt that Sarah Sutton's character was well suited to his Doctor—and Adric, therefore, got blown to smithereens. The crew was joined by Turlough, a public schoolboy initially under the control of the Black Guardian, before Nyssa said her farewells at the end of "Terminus." The story wasn't particularly well-received by the critics, but Nyssa's decision to stay behind was both nicely scripted and acted—another in a line of emotional departures.

The trilogy ended with "Enlightenment," which featured an appearance from Leee John—better known as one third of the soul band Imagination, who enjoyed a couple of hits in the early eighties. Clearly Leee was not his real name: it was (and still is) John McGregor, but I was kind of hoping it was Leeeeeeee and he just got called Leee for short.

Season twenty-one was unusual (but not unique) insofar as it included not only a regeneration but also the inaugural story of the Doctor's new incarnation—the idea presumably was to give viewers a glimpse into the character of the regenerated Time Lord and maintain some level of continuity during the period when the program was off air. Whether or not the idea was a success is a different matter.

It was another reunion-style season, as the Doctor was faced firstly by the Silurians ("Warriors of the Deep") and then the Daleks ("Remembrance of the Daleks"). Nestled in between those adventures were "The Awakening" and "Frontios," the former of which starred Polly James, who is best remembered as Beryl in *The Liver Birds*.

Her fellow flatmate Sandra was played by Nerys Hughes, who had also appeared in the early Peter Davison story "Kinda." And if that wasn't enough, Nerys Hughes had replaced Pauline Collins (who played Dawn in the first series of the sit-com) and she had already portrayed Samantha Briggs in "The Faceless Ones" during the 1960s (as we've seen), before returning as Queen Victoria in the 2006 episode "Tooth and Claw."

"What's got four arms, loves to grab ya?"

"Answer is two Cybermen...."

At the conclusion of "Resurrection of the Daleks," Tegan chose to stay on Earth; so many people had perished and Tegan had seen enough. Traveling with the Doctor was no longer fun, and so, with a firm Aussie handshake, Tegan was gone.

With every change of female companion during the mid-1980s, there seemed to be a reduction in the amount of clothing being worn. The rather demure Nyssa was revealing a "bit of leg" before her departure, and Tegan's short leather miniskirt was soon replaced by the bare flesh of a bikini-clad Peri Brown—a conscious ratings-based decision made from behind the producer's desk I would reckon.

Peri was an American character played by the English-born Nicola Bryant. She joined the fifth Doctor in his penultimate adventure before entering the "Caves of Androzani," where the pair contracted a potentially fatal disease to which the only known cure was the milk of the queen bat. Peri drank the milk and recovered, but the Doctor had to regenerate in order to survive. The new Doctor, played by Colin Baker, became the first incarnation to speak during the episode in which the regeneration sequence of the previous incumbent was filmed: "Change my dear . . . and it seems not a moment too soon."

His character was initially unstable, irritable, and eminently unlikeable, and the sixth Doctor's tenure also included some stories that provoked censure for their use of horror and violence. "Attack of the Cybermen" was one such story, although it should also have been panned for the baggy outfit worn by Michael Kilgarriff's Cybercontroller.

He was reprising a part he had played almost two decades earlier in "Tomb of the Cybermen"—a nice piece of continuity maybe, but robotic aliens with expanding waistlines?

The comeback of the Sontarans later in season twenty-two also marked the return of two familiar faces: Patrick Troughton and Frazer Hines. Reviews of the story (entitled "The Two Doctors") suggest that it was more an attempt to exploit the series' past rather than offer anything new, which was a shame, not least for the legendary Troughton, who passed away just over two years later.

The season ended on a positive note—onscreen at least—with "Revelation of the Daleks." The adventure did receive some criticism for the horror content and yet another appearance of Davros, but the strong performances of Baker and Bryant were recognized and praised.

Behind the scenes, all was not well though. It was announced that season twenty-three would be postponed, and the scheduled themed season known as the "Trial of a Time Lord" (comprising four stories with a total of fourteen episodes) was beset with problems.

BBC Controller Michael Grade had expressed a desire to see more humor injected into the program at the expense of some of the more violent scenes. Writers were paid off, others resigned, and Nicola Bryant was due to leave midway through the season, to be substituted by a character called Mel, who would be played by the established and popular Bonnie Langford.

Although Grade eventually agreed to the production of a further season, it was on the proviso that Colin Baker was replaced. Many fans of the show were furious at the way Baker had been treated, and the actor himself turned down the opportunity to appear in the opening episodes of the next season—and I can't say I blame him.

So, it was farewell to the bright and undoubtedly spirited Peri, and hello to the cheery, optimistic, and intelligent Mel, who could also scream with the very best.

Screaming (or rather "thcweaming") was hardly a new concept for Bonnie Langford, who had played the spoilt, lisping, and unfailingly irritating Violet Elizabeth Bott in the television adaptation of Richmal Crompton's *Just William* stories between 1977 and 1978. She was also associated with another precocious youngster, the ill-fated Lena Zavaroni, and has since enjoyed a successful career on stage, with her most notable role being that of Roxie Hart in several productions of *Chicago*.

I managed to track down Bonnie in February 2011, while she was on a cruise ship bound for Australia. She did e-mail two scanned images, but sadly without the all-important signature, although I did ask—almost pleaded in fact—but sadly to no avail.

VISION OFF

Sylvester McCoy was the actor chosen to replace Colin Baker. I remembered him from the children's program *Vision On*, which was aimed primarily at deaf viewers. The show was presented by Pat Keysell and featured the artist Tony Hart, both of whom passed away aged eighty-three in 2009.

McCoy's first season witnessed a couple of notable guest stars, although some may have been missed: not necessarily because of make-up or costumes but because the series was now being broadcast midweek and was in direct competition with *Coronation Street*. The late Richard Briers is certainly a household name, likewise Ken Dodd—yes *the* Ken Dodd—who played the tattyfilarious Tollmaster in a story called "Delta and the Bannermen."

Tony Osoba and Wanda Ventham have been mentioned earlier in the book and they both returned in season twenty-four. Tony Selby, who featured in the RAF sit-com *Get Some In!* appeared in the series finale "Dragonfire." And another name worthy of mention is Judy Cornwell (who played Maddy in the story "Paradise Towers"), a regular in *Keeping Up Appearances* but who was on our screens more recently as Queenie, mother of (the late) Heather Trott in *Eastenders*.

"Doctor Who and the Curse of the Trotts"—now there's a story I'd pay to see!

Anyway, Mel chose to stay on Iceworld at the end of "Dragonfire"—only her sixth adventure with the Doctor—and was superseded by the young lady pictured on the next page: Sophie Aldred, who played Ace until the show was effectively—if not formally—axed in 1989.

The new season got underway with a trip back to Coal Hill School in November 1963, only this time there was no Ian, Barbara, or Susan, rather two rival Dalek factions on the hunt for a powerful Time Lord device known as the Hand of Omega. The story also featured the junkyard in Totter's Lane—although for some reason the owner's name was spelt "Forman" instead of Foreman.

Sophie Aldred

Incidentally, at the end of the first episode, a Dalek was seen levitating up a flight of stairs: the first time this ability had been demonstrated onscreen. In my youth, I used to get recurrent dreams that Daleks were invading my school, and no matter what I did, my hiding place would always be uncovered and I'd have to run off, with a Dalek in hot pursuit.

But that's not all. Oh no.

Just when I thought I was making good my escape past the junior school classrooms, several Daleks would fly round the corner of the building and start trying to exterminate me as I fled. Apart from the fact that it's not very sporting to shoot a kid in the back, they weren't supposed to be able to levitate, so since when could they bloody fly?

Turning to the present day and what do I see? Airborne Daleks everywhere! Hang on a second, wasn't that my idea?

Eventually, the Hand was captured by the imperial Daleks and the Emperor was revealed as Davros, but his desire to use the device resulted in the vaporization of the Daleks' home planet Skaro. The Doctor then caused the Dalek Supreme to self-destruct, and everyone went home happy—well, perhaps with the exception of Davros. Ace showed herself to be streetwise and outwardly tough: she was also fiercely loyal to the Doctor (whom she called "Professor").

Next came "The Happiness Patrol," in which being miserable resulted in death at the hands of a Bertie Bassett lookalike.

Bizarre.

Doctor Who duly reached its twenty-fifth anniversary with a return of the Cybermen in what I have read is a pretty weak adventure entitled "Silver Nemesis." However, the season ended with "The Greatest Show in the Galaxy," which featured sinister clowns and "gods" in the form of a family that craved entertainment and summarily destroyed anything they didn't enjoy.

Best not send them a copy of this book then.

Season twenty-six would revolve more around Ace, as the series' title character manipulated events in the background rather than taking center stage. The opening story, "Battlefield," saw Nicholas Courtney reprise his role as Lethbridge-Stewart and marked a return for Jean Marsh (as Morgaine), who had played Sara Kingdom in "The Daleks Master Plan" as well as appearing in the 1965 historical tale "The Crusade."

And now, from Norwich, it's the *Sale of the Century*!

Actually, it was "The Curse of Fenric" and the location was Northumberland (supposedly) during World War II, but there in the guise of Reverend Wainwright was none other than Nicholas Parsons. Also in the cast was Anne Reid, who would reappear in the David Tennant tale "Smith and Jones" as Florence Finnegan, a blood-sucking alien—a far cry from *Coronation Street* where, as Val Barlow, Anne met an untimely demise when she was fatally zapped by a hairdryer.

All of which brings us to the final story of the original series, ironically called "Survival." Coincidentally, there was also a return to contemporary London, right back where things had started over quarter of a century earlier.

Having overcome the Master and the Cheetah people, who came from the Cheetah planet and looked like . . . —go on, have a wild guess—the Doctor and Ace turned and walked off into the distance.

The Doctor's final speech was over-dubbed when it became apparent there would be no season twenty-seven, and this is how the story ended: "There are worlds out there where the sky is burning, the sea's asleep and the rivers dream; people made of smoke and cities made of song. Somewhere there's danger, somewhere there's injustice and somewhere the tea is getting cold.

"Come on Ace, we've got work to do."

Sophie Aldred was born in Greenwich in August 1962, and was cast as Ace four years after graduating from the University of Manchester; she has subsequently worked as a presenter and voice-over artist. Sophie married presenter Vince Henderson in 1997, and the couple have two sons named Adam and William. This section of *Doctor Who*'s history ends with one more photograph of Sophie as Ace.

Sophie Aldred

SAVING GRACE

In May 1996, a television film based on *Doctor Who* was broadcast—initially in Canada, a couple of days before being aired in America, and just over two weeks before British audiences had the chance to see the new offering.

The movie was an attempt at reviving the series; the intention was that the film would be a sort of pilot for a new program, which would have been produced in the States.

Whilst the film was a success on this side of the water, it was less well received in America; no new series was commissioned and this would prove to be the first and only appearance of Paul McGann as the Doctor. The hour and a half episode also showcased Daphne Ashbrook as Dr. Grace Holloway.

I did a sort of synopsis of the movie in the second edition—something I'm not going to repeat here—suffice to say that the storyline featured both the Master and the Eye of Harmony, both previously integral parts of "The Deadly Assassin." The Master was played by Julia Roberts's brother Eric (his wife Eliza was also in the film), and this would be the last appearance of the Doctor's nemesis until the 2007 episode "Utopia," when the character was portrayed by Derek Jacobi and, after regenerating, John Simm (the fifth and sixth actors respectively to take on the role). There were also echoes of "Spearhead from Space," as the respective Doctors "acquired" clothing from a hospital (viz. Matt Smith in "The Eleventh Hour" as well).

During the movie, the Doctor kissed Grace—and we're not talking cheek-pecking—and this was arguably the first time in the program's history when the Time Lord's sexuality was explored. The twenty-first century was looming, audiences were moving with times, and *Doctor Who* needed to do the same. Certainly, critical reaction to the bond between the Doctor and Grace was extremely favorable, and it seems clear that the film laid the foundation for future Doctor-companion relationships.

The British transmission of the movie took place on Monday, May 27, 1996, and nine million viewers tuned in—the highest audience for any drama that particular week. At the end of the broadcast, there was a dedication to Jon Pertwee, who had passed away seven days earlier, two months before his seventy-seventh birthday.

And this is the wonderful photo I received from Daphne Ashbrook—all the way from America!

Daphne Ashbrook

Daphne has a whole string of television acting credits to her name: *Cold Case*, *Murder She Wrote*, *The O.C.*, *CSI*, and, perhaps most memorably, *Star Trek: Deep Space Nine* as Melora. It's (subjectively) interesting to note that of the twelve people to have appeared in both the *Doctor Who* television series and one of the *Star Trek* franchises, Daphne is the only American and the only woman.

If you want to know the others, you should have bought the second edition!

Oh go on then: Barrie Ingham, Olaf Pooley, Guy Siner, John Franklyn-Robbins, Deep Roy, Christopher Neame, Maurice Roëves, Simon Pegg, father and son Morgan and Mark Sheppard, and Noel Clarke.

THE WAIT IS OVER

Notwithstanding the 1996 movie, there was a hiatus of some sixteen years between "Survival" and the first episode of the all-new series.

There were novels, plays, and audio stories, but not the series that so many fans had hoped for. However in 2003, the BBC announced a new in-house production that was being led by writer Russell T. Davies and Julie Gardner, who was Head of Drama at BBC Cymru Wales.

The new Doctor was unveiled as Christopher Eccleston, an accomplished stage and screen actor, and his companion was to be the former pop star Billie Piper, whose character (Rose Tyler) lived in London and worked in a department store.

The hugely anticipated first episode, simply entitled "Rose," aired on March 26, 2005, and was watched by over ten million viewers (at its peak)—more than *Ant & Dec's Saturday Night Takeaway*, which was on ITV at the same time.

It was a triumphant return. A forty-five minute story that successfully managed to introduce the new Doctor, Rose, her boyfriend Mickey Smith (Noel Clarke), and her mother Jackie (Camille Coduri, below), as well as

Camille Coduri

featuring a close encounter with the Nestene Consciousness and the Autons, last seen in the early part of Jon Pertwee's tenure over three decades earlier.

Eccleston's Doctor combined the dark and serious with instant shifts to levity and comedy. He would only play the Time Lord for one series, but the fact that he was almost instantly accepted as the Doctor is a credit to the scriptwriters and the way that Eccleston characterized the role.

But, I would have to say that Billie Piper was the star of the show. Seldom has *Doctor Who* been graced by a performer of such talent, and Billie's portrayal of shopgirl-turned-time-traveler is—for what my opinion is worth—one of the major factors in the incredible success the program has achieved over the past eight years.

Obviously, given the advances in technology as well as what was probably a proportionally larger budget, it was always likely that the new series would look spectacular and that the "original" would perhaps suffer by comparison. But for me it wasn't so much the assessment of differences, it was simply about enjoying the current version of a program I had loved watching as a kid—only now I could have a glass or two of wine at the same time.

Even so, the effects were absolutely amazing—like when Mickey was "eaten" by a plastic rubbish bin; now that was wheelie clever.

Rose decided to leave Mickey and her humdrum life behind, and the Doctor whisked her forward to the year five billion—I've no idea how many zeros that is—where she witnessed the natural end of the planet Earth before rematerializing in Victorian Cardiff and joining forces with Charles Dickens to investigate the mysterious walking dead. This particular tale featured Eve Myles, who played a servant named Gwyneth; Eve would later be cast as Gwen Cooper in the *Doctor Who* spin-off *Torchwood*.

A two-part story followed ("Aliens of London" and "World War Three") and introduced a race named the Slitheen, who could squeeze their bodies into human "suits": their identities only being revealed once a zip in the forehead was pulled—oh and they farted all the time too.

Just out of curiosity, I've been checking my forehead; there is no sign of a zip, so I can safely conclude I am not a Slitheen—I simply have a wind problem.

Anyway, another character who, whilst not a companion, would appear semi-regularly was MP Harriet Jones—yes we know who you are—portrayed by Penelope Wilton, with whom I share a birthday (the date, not the year).

Then, on April 30, 2005, came the episode most *Doctor Who* fans had been waiting for. Producers clearly went to extraordinary lengths to keep the identity of the Doctor's adversaries a secret: they called the episode "Dalek."

The action took place in 2012, inside an underground bunker in Utah, owned by the wealthy Henry van Statten, a collector of alien artifacts. Van Statten's personal assistant (Diana) Goddard was played by Anna-Louise Plowman, who had also been on our television screens as Annalese Carson in the ever-watchable *Holby City*.

Back underground, the pride of Van Statten's collection was a Metaltron. Actually, it was a Dalek, but you can't blame the bloke for not knowing. The machine was chained up and effectively dormant, but when it was touched by Rose it absorbed her DNA and came back to life—and it wasn't a happy chappy.

The Dalek discovered it was the last of its race and did a bit of exterminating for old time's sake, but spared Rose's life—courtesy of the human DNA—in return for the release from the vault where it had been held. Rose ultimately managed to convince the Dalek that it could have freedom; it blasted a hole in the ceiling, opened its casing to the sunlight, and self-destructed, duly freeing itself from everything that the Daleks stood for.

Rather than continuing the seasonal numbers used up until 1989—this would have been season twenty-seven—the new format was identified as series one, and a genuinely chilling moment was just around the corner.

The two-part story "The Empty Child" and "The Doctor Dances" was set in the Second World War and featured a young boy wearing a gas mask, as well as other zombie-type people, all of whom were constantly asking for their "mummy."

Inside a hospital ward, Dr. Constantine (Richard Wilson) watched over apparent corpses, complete with gas masks that would momentarily reanimate if there was a loud noise. Just after Dr. Constantine explained that every patient had identical injuries and the gas masks seemed to actually be part of the victim's faces, he too began to change.

By now, the regular cast had been joined by John Barrowman as Capt. Jack Harkness: a Time Agent and all-action former con man, who would acquire the gift—or perhaps the curse—of immortality. The adult-targeted series *Torchwood* would later be built around Barrowman's character.

The series concluded with another two-part adventure, "Bad Wolf" and "The Parting of the Ways." The former featured android-hosted reality television shows, all with deadly consequences, and the latter was another encounter with the Daleks, which ended with the Doctor's regeneration.

Curiously, this was the first time the Doctor had regenerated standing up, but the fourth time the change had taken place inside the TARDIS ("The Tenth Planet," "The Caves of Androzani," and "Time and the Rani" being the other three).

The second series—cleverly called series two—began with a special show on Christmas Day 2005 ("The Christmas Invasion"), which was David Tennant's first full adventure as the eponymous Doctor. The subsequent tale, "School Reunion," reunited the Doctor with Sarah Jane Smith and K-9, and there were some touching scenes between Time Lord and past companion. By May 2006, Tennant was very much established in the role, and it was time for the return of an old foe.

"Rise of the Cybermen" was followed by "The Age of Steel" as the new-look twenty-first century Cybermen stomped onto our screens for the first time since 1988. A number of previous stories had seen the cyborgs aided by a human ally—Tobias Vaughan in "The Invasion" (1968) and Kellman in "Revenge of the Cybermen" in 1975 for example—and here it was the wheelchair-bound John Lumic, played by Roger Lloyd-Pack. Coincidentally, Tennant and Lloyd-Pack had worked together on the movie *Harry Potter and the Goblet of Fire*.

Six episodes later came a two-part story that witnessed a climactic battle between the Cybermen and the Daleks—the first time the two races had been paired as direct enemies in the show's history. This two-parter also featured Rose's "death"—she actually survived, but in a parallel world. "The Army of Ghosts" set the scene, with blurred apparitions being revealed as a mass army of Cybermen; meanwhile, a mysterious sphere opened to reveal . . . Daleks.

The adventure unfolded in "Doomsday," as the two alien powers fought for supremacy. Inside the sphere was the Genesis Ark, which turned out to be a prison ship built by the Time Lords, holding millions of Daleks. And things looked pretty desperate as the inhabitants of Earth were faced with extermination, deletion, or conversion.

The Doctor found a way to reopen a breach across the void between universes, but as the alien threat was being sucked into the void, Rose let go of a magnetic clamp that was keeping her out of harm's way. Thankfully, her "dead" father miraculously appeared to snatch Rose in the nick of time, transporting her into a parallel universe.

The threat was ultimately averted, but the Doctor and Rose were now separated. Soon after, Rose had a dream in which the Doctor was calling her; she made the journey to a remote bay in Norway, where the Doctor reappeared—albeit as a projection—and the pair shared a truly heart-wrenching farewell. Speaking as someone who blubs at the father-daughter platform reunion in *The Railway Children*, an emotional scene such as this was bound to set me off—and it did . . . several times.

Billie Piper's departure brought an end to one of the best ever *Doctor Who* pairings. In my opinion, the only two combinations that can arguably rival the tenth Doctor and Rose are Patrick Troughton's incarnation and Jamie, or Tom Baker's portrayal alongside Sarah Jane Smith.

There's not a great deal anyone can really add about the life and career of a young woman who only reached her thirtieth birthday in September 2012, but . . . Billie's debut single *Because We Want To* went straight into the UK charts at number one, making her the youngest artist to achieve the feat. Her acting career has ranged from science fiction to Shakespeare, and includes roles such as Hannah Baxter (Belle de Jour) in the *Secret Diary of a Call Girl* and the less well-known, but wonderful, portrayal of Betty in Kay Mellor's 2010 drama, *A Passionate Woman*.

Billie Piper

She's been married twice and has two sons with her current husband Laurence Fox—all that as well as traveling to the farthest reaches of the universe in a battered old blue police box.

The role of her replacement, Martha Jones, was taken by Freema Agyeman, who had briefly appeared in "The Army of Ghosts" as Adeola Oshodi, a Torchwood employee who was "upgraded" and effectively killed by the Cybermen. "Doomsday" marked the first contemporary appearance for Torchwood, although the organization eventually seen in the series of the same name was much removed from this original concept.

Viewers would have to wait to see Martha's first story, as the end of "Doomsday" led directly into what would be another Christmas special, "The Runaway Bride," featuring Catherine Tate as future companion Donna Noble.

Series three (or season twenty-nine if you prefer) began on March 31, 2007, with an episode entitled "Smith & Jones." The story revolved around the transportation of a hospital to the Moon by the imposing rhino-like ("rhinocerotic," he noted smugly) Judoon, but it was essentially a vehicle to introduce Martha Jones.

During the episode, medical student Martha and the Time Lord shared a kiss that the Doctor explained away as a genetic transfer—I'd use that line myself if I had my time again!—but by the end of the story, the hospital was safely restored to its rightful place and the Doctor had a new companion.

Rose Tyler was gentle and sympathetic: sharp-witted and courageous in the face of an alien threat. Martha was equally brave as well as being outgoing and intelligent, but Rose was probably the more likely to kill one of the Doctor's enemies. Both had strong feelings for the Doctor; Rose's jealous streak surfaced when the Doctor was initially reunited with Sarah Jane, and Martha revealed a similar trait in the two-parter "Human Nature" and "Family of Blood."

Rose proved that she was willing to make the ultimate sacrifice in order to give the Doctor a chance of saving the planet ("Doomsday"), and Martha would also show herself to be selfless in her efforts to care for or help the Doctor.

The series' third story was a throwback to a bygone era with the return of the Macra: giant crablike ("cancrine" . . . smug overload imminent) creatures that had enjoyed one previous outing ("The Macra Terror") in the 1960s. The forty year interval between appearances of any character or alien race was the longest in *Doctor Who* history. It may have been subsequently exceeded by the Great Intelligence (viz. "The Web of Fear" and "The Snowmen") although there is maybe a distinction to be drawn between the tangible and the invisible.

After what I thought was a substandard Dalek story set in 1930s Manhattan, the next adventure, "The Lazarus Experiment" added another name to the list of performers who had appeared in both *Coronation Street* and *Doctor Who*: namely Thelma (Mavis) Barlow.

"Human Nature" and "The Family of Blood" were set in 1913 and saw the Doctor change his DNA to become human to hide from a race of aliens called "the Family," who had been pursuing the TARDIS. The Doctor's consciousness was locked inside a fob watch as the Family possessed the locals and closed in on their intended prey.

Ultimately, the Doctor was maneuvered into a situation where he faced a choice between living his life as John Smith, or reverting back to being a Time Lord and dealing with the menace of the Family and their army of animated scarecrows. He chose the latter, defeated the Family, and gave each member the immortality they craved, but in a cold, almost callous manner.

The watch ended up in the possession of a schoolboy named Tim Latimer, and with the alien threat averted, the episode moved on to show a clip from the First World War—which had started just a few months after the story was set—and depicted Tim and boys from his school fighting a very different enemy.

The action then cut to the present day to show an elderly Latimer attending an Armistice Day parade, still holding the watch—it was a poignant end to an excellent piece of drama.

The great stories continued with "Blink," which is reviewed in the all-new chapter that follows, and the series ended with an epic three-part encounter with a newly regenerated Master (initially in the guise of Professor Yana and later as Prime Minister Harry Saxon).

Anyway, here is a signed photo of Freema Agyeman to round off the chapter. Freema was born in March 1979, and I've read that she is of Ghanaian and Iranian heritage. Since *Doctor Who*, Freema has played Alesha Phillips in *Law and Order UK* and Jenny Walsh in the remake of the cult series *Survivors*—albeit briefly . . . she was killed in the first episode.

Freema Agyeman

READ IT AND WEEP

This third edition is the first to have featured any semblance of a synopsis and review of one of the "new" stories. Plot memories and opinions will be fresher in the mind, and the fact that I can't hide my points of view behind the thin veneer of passing time is a bit of a worry if the truth be told, but I'm facing the challenge head on.

"Blink" was penned by Steven Moffat and was first broadcast on 9 June, 2007. It starred the BAFTA award-winner Carey Mulligan alongside former *Casualty* nurse—and one of my favorite actresses—Lucy Gaskell as Sally Sparrow and Kathy Nightingale respectively.

The basic premise of the plot is that stone statues are actually an alien race capable, by touch, of transporting people back in time. The "victim" would essentially live to death and the Weeping Angels would then gain power from the potential energy of the lost future years.

The action gets underway in a creepy abandoned house, Wester Drumlins. Sally Sparrow has broken in—although it wasn't particularly difficult—and is taking pictures when she is drawn to some writing behind a ripped piece of wallpaper.

As Sally tears the paper away from the wall, a message is revealed, mentioning Sally by name and encouraging her to "duck," which she does in the nick of time as a rock flies across the room.

I did have a bit of a problem with this scene insofar as the paper came off the wall in huge chunks that were the perfect size to uncover the warning underneath. Now, most times I've tried to strip wallpaper, it's come off in tiny pieces and I've ended up with a scraper or some steam contraption to get the job done. That said, I suppose the episode wouldn't have had quite the same effect if Sally's frantic scraping had only exposed the "d" of "duck" before the stone smacked her in the back of the head.

Sally heads to Kathy's flat where she spots a number of television and computer screens showing paused images of the Doctor—she also gets a pretty good view of Kathy's naked brother Laurence (Larry), but fortunately that's of no relevance to the story.

Sally returns (along with Kathy) to Wester Drumlins the following day. She points out that she loves the derelict house because it makes her feel sad—apparently sad is happy for deep people! Sally notices that the stone angel, its eyes obscured by cupped hands, appears to have moved since the previous night, and the pair are soon startled by a knock at the door. Sally answers, Kathy hides, and the stealthy progress of the Angel towards its unsuspecting victim is cleverly filmed.

The visitor offers Sally a handwritten letter, which she opens. It is from Katherine Wainwright (née Nightingale): it claims it was "mere minutes since we last spoke," and it also includes a photograph of a woman whose clothing is from a bygone era but whose face is identical to her friend. Off camera, a sudden noise signals that the Angel has reached Kathy—in contemporary times, she has simply disappeared, but she is in fact alive and well, albeit understandably surprised, having "arrived" in a field in Hull in 1920.

I'm not sure how accurate a representation it was of the East Riding city, but it wasn't raining, and I'd suggest that's a bad start.

Sally tries to find Kathy, but comes across more Angels, one of whom is holding a key, which she snatches. She discovers Kathy's gravestone, with her birthdate inscribed as 1902: "You told him you were eighteen, you lying cow!"

In a local DVD store (where Larry Nightingale works), Sally again sees the "Easter egg" extras that have been located on seventeen separate DVDs. Larry gives Sally a list, which she puts in her pocket but doesn't read.

The plot lines are converging nicely. Sally is being bombarded by the unexplained, but is coping well in the circumstances. She heads to the police station, where she meets DI Billy Shipton—unprofessionalism personified: "Time is short and you are hot!" Sally is shown vehicles abandoned near the house, whose owners and passengers have mysteriously disappeared, and she also spots the TARDIS, only realizing once she has left Shipton that she probably has the key in her pocket.

In the brief time it takes to return, Shipton gets sent back to 1969 where he encounters Martha and the Doctor—complete with his "timey-wimey detector that goes ding when there's stuff." Shipton needs to take a message to Sally, but he's got quite a while to wait.

Sally gets a phone call from the now elderly Shipton, whose life is nearly at an end. It transpires he left the police and worked in video publishing .

. . ahhh, so it was Shipton who added the Easter eggs, and as for the list of DVDs that was still in Sally's pocket, well they represented the sum total of her collection. So there's no time to waste.

Back at "Scooby Doo's house" with Larry, the Doctor's full recording is played and Sally finds that she's completing the missing half of the conversation even though she initially can't understand how the Doctor can "know what I'm going to say, forty years before I say it."

"Thirty-eight," corrects the Time Lord.

The Doctor explains that the Angels are only statues when you see them—they simply don't exist when being observed. Sally needs to get the TARDIS back to 1969, but as the conversation and transcript abruptly end, it is clear that the Angels are coming.

The Doctor's words of warning couldn't be more stark: "Don't blink, don't even blink; blink and you're dead. They are fast, faster than you could believe. Don't turn your back; don't look away and *don't* blink."

Easy to say, but a whole lot harder when a set of very sharp-looking stone teeth are being bared right in front of your face.

The conundrum is cleverly resolved. Sally and Larry manage to enter the TARDIS, which is encircled by four Angels. The TARDIS dematerializes leaving the two youngsters behind and seemingly in major trouble, but the disappearance of the solid object has resulted in each of the Angels looking at the one opposite, instantly turning one and all to stone.

Moving forward in time, Sally is running a high street shop (with Larry), a taxi pulls up outside, and out step the Doctor and Martha. Sally goes to talk to the Time Lord, who doesn't recognize her because whatever happens hasn't . . . yet . . . sort of thing. But, Sally hands the Doctor all the documents he will need for when he's transported back to 1969, and from the initial incredulity at seeing her name written on the wall of an abandoned house, comes Sally's realization that she has simply fulfilled her destiny.

Although the Doctor and Martha weren't onscreen for long, I must admit that the sight of Martha walking down the street carrying a case of arrows over her shoulder . . . well it sent me all of a quiver.

Really that should have been that, but the episode ended with a totally unnecessary montage of various statues, gargoyles and the like, embellished with dramatic music, presumably so the viewer knew the Angels would be returning. It didn't spoil the story, but it certainly didn't add to it either.

Anyway, what is interesting is just how much content the current writers and producers could fit into forty-five minutes. "Blink" is one example of a single drama that is played out at a decent pace, builds atmosphere, includes excellent effects yet doesn't scrimp on character portrayal or development, despite the obvious time constraints. I wonder—in fact I dread to think—how many twenty-five minute parts this could have been padded out to in the late 60s or early 70s?

As you'd expect, Carey Mulligan and Lucy Gaskell are superb, and the limited—although to an extent repetitive—appearance of the Doctor actually enhances the drama; how can he save the day when he isn't even there? But clearly the central focus of "Blink" is the Weeping Angels.

Or at least it's supposed to be.

On paper, it is hard to visualize how an unspeaking and inanimate creature could work onscreen, but it does . . . or at least it did. Putting the majority of the Angels' menace in the minds of the audience is an excellent concept; the inference of movement and the aggressive facial expressions that suddenly appear as they draw in on their prey . . . well it is all pretty impressive really.

My issue isn't with "Blink"—it's a compelling piece of television—it's actually the fact that the Angels would return . . . and return again. Looking forward, although the eventual manner of Amy and Rory's departure was incredibly moving, the subsequent appearances of the Angels simply didn't work for me. A child at a pantomime will ultimately tire of shouting he or she's "behind you," the effect of unseen movement descended from the sinister to the wholly expected, and any resulting lack of tension—perceived or otherwise—simply detracted from the story.

The concluding question is, therefore, does "Blink" work *because* of the Weeping Angels, or is the story strong enough that the alien foe becomes largely irrelevant?

I would lean towards the latter, but I wouldn't lean far enough to fall over and agree entirely. The Angels are fine but the narrative is brilliant, so whilst I feel the Angels do, on this occasion, add something to the drama, I don't believe they are capable as a standalone "monster" of sustaining a weaker story.

Along with the Matt Smith tale "The Lodger," "Blink" is definitely one of my absolute favorite stories from the new era. Good enough to be different and different enough to be good—speaking subjectively of course.

But whether or not you agree, at least the chapter will end well. Very well indeed, in fact, with a signed still from "Blink," which I received from the lovely Lucy Gaskell.

Wigan-born Lucy is married to Mark Bonnar (who appeared in the Matt Smith two-part adventure "The Rebel Flesh" and "The Almost People") and she didn't just send this photo, there were two others of her playing the part of Kirsty Clements in *Casualty* as well as a handwritten letter. Lucy didn't play a companion, but her photo simply has to be included.

Lucy Gaskell

OI! WATCH IT SPACEMAN!

There was a rare treat in the 2007 Christmas special: a guest appearance by Kylie Minogue. The one-off episode was entitled "Voyage of the Damned" and was based around the ill-fated ocean liner *RMS Titanic*, whose maiden voyage in 1912 didn't go particularly well. Now though, Titanic was a luxury space cruiser, and the Doctor was faced with trying to prevent a sabotaged ship from colliding with the planet Earth.

Kylie played a waitress named Astrid Peth (the fact that Astrid was an anagram of TARDIS was apparently a coincidence), who gave her life to kill former cruise-line owner Max Capricorn, who had plotted the destruction of the vessel using angel-faced robots called the Host. So why did she sacrifice herself?

Je ne sais pas pourquoi.

The cast included Gray O'Brien who, as Tony Gordon, was responsible for a fair amount of evil-doing in *Coronation Street*. And, while we're on the subject of soap killers, the Doctor's new companion Donna Noble appeared in "Partners in Crime," the story that followed "Voyage of the Damned," albeit four months later. Donna's original appearance was in an earlier Christmas special, "The Runaway Bride," in which her intended husband Lance was played by Don Gilet, who would later become the mass-murdering, manic-staring, chin-stroking bible-basher Lucas Johnson in *Eastenders*.

I guess I wasn't alone in wondering if Catherine Tate was the right choice to play a *Doctor Who* companion; she was so well known for characters in various comedy sketches. But, if you want to judge her straight acting skills, you only need to watch her performance in "Journey's End"—the moment when Donna realized the Doctor would have to wipe her mind to save her life.

It was genuinely moving.

Anyway, after a journey back to Pompeii in 79AD—at the time when Mount Vesuvius was about to erupt and destroy the city—Donna encountered a raced called the Ood: weird-looking enslaved creatures who, once freed, could start to sing again.

I'm not sure exactly what the Ood's song was, but I think it might be that Nolan's classic *I'm in the Ood for Dancing*. Or—and this is my wife Elaine's suggestion—*Ood Do You Think You Are* by the Spice Girls.

Hers is better isn't it?

Donna initially displayed a sharp tongue and a volatile temper, but whilst she maintained her dry sense of humor, her compassion soon started to shine through. She was smarter and far more important than she realized, but Donna couldn't see past the "temp from Chiswick."

Digressing slightly, the story entitled "The Doctor's Daughter," which was transmitted in May 2008, featured Georgia Moffett—and yes I got a signed photo—as the eponymous daughter Jenny. What is interesting is that Georgia's real life father is the Time Lord's fifth incarnation Peter Davison, and her husband is David Tennant, Doctor number ten.

Georgia Moffett

Georgia's appearance in *Doctor Who* was not the first by a child of the program's lead actor; that honor actually fell to David Troughton, who appeared as Private Moor in his father Patrick's final story, "The War Games," in 1969, not long after an uncredited part in "The Enemy of the World." David's most notable role would be that of King Peladon in the Jon Pertwee story "The Curse of Peladon," and he later—much later—played Professor Hobbes in the 2008 tale "Midnight."

Back to Donna Noble, and the character took center stage in Russell T. Davies's superb "Turn Left," in which the simple action of turning a car right instead of left at a junction was the catalyst for a remarkable series of events, all of which related to previous *Doctor Who* stories.

In the alternate history: The Doctor died in "The Runaway Bride;" Martha and Sarah Jane both perished when the hospital was transported to the Moon ("Smith and Jones"); London was destroyed by a nuclear explosion after the Titanic space cruiser crashed into Buckingham Palace; and Gwen Cooper and the Torchwood team gave their lives to save Earth from a toxic fog activated by the Sontarans ("The Poison Sky").

"Turn Left" certainly rates as one of Catherine Tate's best performances, and the story also featured the first significant reappearance of Billie Piper as Rose Tyler. The scene was now set for the dramatic series finale ("The Stolen Earth" and "Journey's End").

The big climax came with Earth and twenty-six other planets being transported across the cosmos to a place where their alignment would create enough scientific mumbo jumbo to detonate a reality bomb that would destroy . . . well, pretty much everything. Davros and the Daleks were behind the dastardly scheme, and they were faced by not one but two seemingly identical Doctors, along with a veritable plethora of companions, assistants, and family—including various members of Torchwood.

The bomb was tested on a small huddle of humans, one of whom was instantly recognizable as Gita from *Eastenders*, and all she could do was silently mouth the name "Sanjaaaaayyy" as she was obliterated into a pile of nothingness.

It was Donna who saved the day though, becoming part Time Lord after touching a case that contained the Doctor's severed hand—I'm trying to keep this simple. Donna was able to stop the reality bomb and disable the Daleks, but she was not able to cope with the mental ability of a Time Lord, and the Doctor had to remove all memory of their shared adventures to save her life. As I said a few pages ago, it was a poignant moment, wonderfully acted.

The Tennant era eventually ended on New Year's Day 2010, in a two-part story called "The End of Time." John Simm reprised his role as the Master, while Donna, her mother Sylvia (Jacqueline King), and her grandfather Wilfred Mott (Bernard Cribbens) all returned, as Tennant's Doctor bowed out of the series after nearly five years of almost unprecedented success in the role.

Bernard Cribbens is a man with a rare association with *Doctor Who*. Back in 1966, a youthful Cribbens played Special Constable Tom Campbell in the film *Daleks - Invasion Earth 2150AD*, the second of the big screen *Doctor Who* adaptations starring Peter Cushing. Tom was essentially the movie's Ian Chesterton; he stumbled upon the TARDIS believing it to be a real telephone box while attempting to foil a robbery.

After a gap spanning some forty-one years, Bernard was cast as Wilfred Mott in the 2007 Christmas special, "Voyage of the Damned." Cribbens return in the 2008 season opener "Partners in Crime," when it was established that Wilfred was Donna Noble's grandfather—I have read that the character replaced Donna's father Geoff Noble, following the untimely death of actor Howard Attfield.

As for Donna Noble, or more particularly Catherine Tate, the photo that follows was received in February 2013. I was probably more surprised

Catherine Tate

to receive this more than any other picture because I'd last written to Catherine some two years earlier! Good things come to he who waits!

Already a well-known performer, thanks to her comedy sketch show, Catherine Tate was thirty-eight when she made her first appearance as Donna. According to my calculations, this makes her the oldest female companion to date: Jacqueline Hill and Daphne Ashbrook were both in their thirties, and Caroline John was just a few months short of her thirtieth birthday. Alex Kingston was in her mid-forties when she joined the program—you can argue her companion status amongst yourselves or simply move on to the next chapter!

MATT FINISH

We're entering the home straight now, with the current Doctor (played by Matt Smith) and the first of his female sidekicks, Amelia (Amy) Pond.

I must admit that I thought I would struggle to get a reply from actress Karen Gillan—perhaps more so than some of the former assistants—purely because of the volume of mail she was likely to receive, as she was the still the Doctor's companion when I wrote to her. As it turned out, Karen replied not once but twice, and the first of those photographs will appear very soon.

Karen was born in November 1987, pretty much halfway between my two daughters. Statuesque, with striking red hair, it's no real surprise that Karen's CV includes modeling work. But on the acting front, the role of Amy Pond was Karen's big breakthrough—although she had made a number of minor television appearances after leaving her native Inverness for London's bright lights and the Italia Conti Academy of Theatre Arts (alumni of which include William Hartnell and Bonnie Langford).

Interestingly, one of those bit parts had actually been in *Doctor Who*, as a member of the sisterhood in the David Tennant story "The Fires of Pompeii." Her first appearance as the "grown-up" Amy was far more memorable. She was dressed in a police uniform and her character's job as a kiss-o-gram gave Karen (and her legs) plenty of media exposure.

At this point, I would mention my hope that Matt Smith's portrayal of the Doctor will be accepted as one of the classic characterizations of the Time Lord. I may be biased, but I see a lot of Patrick Troughton in the charming eccentricity of the eleventh Doctor: quirky, funny at times, but smart and obscure enough to mask his knowledge if necessary.

Smith's frantic and nonsensical manner in "The Eleventh Hour" was pure Troughton, and writers seem to have paid homage to that era in "Victory of the Daleks," during which we hear the grating alien voice declare: "I am your soldier," a thinly disguised reference to the "I am your servant" sham from the 1966 story "Power of the Daleks."

Karen Gillan

I find it hard to fault Smith, but I do think that it may ultimately be David Tennant's interpretation that will be considered the one against which other actors are judged. For me though, Matt Smith is an absolute natural in the role, whereas as Tennant often needed all of his considerable talent to "overact" the part.

I'm not saying Tennant wasn't good—he was very good indeed—I simply think Matt Smith is better.

I fear I may end up being slightly controversial here, but I think the Tennant era generally benefited from stronger stories. Recently there have been so many intertwined plot lines, and the current production team is simply trying to squeeze too much action into every episode—slightly ironic given the ridiculous amount of padding that was seen in decades gone by. Plots become confusing as a result and... read on if you don't believe me...

Rory (Arthur Darvill) gets turned to dust... wait, no he's fine... phew it was just a dream... now he's been shot... and erased from existence... that seems a bit final... but no, he's returned... as an Auton... oh dear, that's disappeared as well... but woohoo Rory's back!... oh no, he's been shot again... and drowned... and taken off life support... that's a blow....

But eventually [*spoiler alert*] Amy finds Rory in the shower; he's turned into Bobby Ewing and everything was just one long dream.

As for Amy Pond, she was every inch the twenty-first century companion; the surprisingly mature young Amelia (played by Karen Gillan's real-life cousin Caitlin Blackwood) grew into the feisty Amy, who was occasionally flippant in the face of danger, but her outer toughness hid a loyal and compassionate young woman.

At the time, much was written about Amy's choice in clothes, but her short skirts were nothing else but the fashion of the day; Zoë's outfits were arguably more risqué—and for a highly qualified scientist, Liz Shaw wasn't averse to showing a bit of leg either.

December 25, 2010, saw the broadcast of the sixth Christmas special since *Doctor Who* was revived. "A Christmas Carol" was transmitted both here and in the United States on the same day—the first time this had happened.

I could try and summarize the plot, but I'm not going to. Suffice to say there is another appearance of the fez ("I wear a fez now, fezzes are cool" —"The Big Bang"), there was a shark, and also a chance to see and hear the beautiful Katherine Jenkins, who played the cryogenically challenged Aligail Pettigrew, her first major acting role.

And before you ask. . .

Katherine Jenkins

Series six proved to be action-packed and confusing in equal measure. For me, the stories remained weaker, or perhaps more complicated, than the Tennant era, and I found it hard to accept the idea that Amy's TARDIS-conceived daughter Melody could, would, and did grow up to become River Song.

The following series was arguably an improvement, and included "Asylum of the Daleks," ostensibly a means to introduce Jenna-Louise Coleman as (Clara) Oswin Oswald, a human who had been converted into a Dalek in every way except mentally. Three episodes later came "The Power of Three," an enjoyable mixture of the comic and serious, which starred Jemma Redgrave as UNIT scientific advisor Kate Stewart, the daughter of the late Brigadier Alistair Lethbridge-Stewart—a nice touch with actor Nicholas Courtney having passed away in February 2011.

Series seven also included the departure of Amy and Rory at the literal hands of the Weeping Angels. The story was well devised—particularly the ending—and whilst I suppose that most of the attention will, perhaps unsurprisingly, be focused on Karen Gillan, Arthur Darvill's portrayal of Rory Williams should not be underestimated. Sometimes three isn't a crowd, and I have a feeling that in years to come, viewers will look back on these two companions as one of the best pairings in the show's history.

I wasn't too sure about returning to Manhattan—where the Daleks had already visited during Tennant's tenure—but that said, given the Angels' ability to dump their victims back in time, the story could easily have been called "Manhattan Transfer" (and subtitled "Rat-ti-tat-ti-tat"—one for the forty-somethings).

As far as the ending was concerned, the twist that saw Rory and Amy transported several decades into the past was really cleverly constructed. You assumed something like that might happen, but the writers were insightful enough to create the "happy ever after" scenario before the Angel suddenly struck. What these final scenes showed was not only the acting talents of Smith and Gillan but the obvious chemistry between the pair: great, emotive performances, and I certainly wouldn't be surprised if the tears they shed were actually real.

All of which brings us to Clara Oswald, the final companion to feature in our near fifty-year-trip back in time.

The former *Emmerdale* and *Waterloo Road* actress Jenna Louise-Coleman is (as I write) relatively new to our screens, and her character is

Karen Gillan

still to be fully developed. But, this is what Jenna-Louise said about her new role in April 2013: "Clara looks a little bit cutesy but she's got biker boots on. She's the kind of girl who [*looks like she*] sits in a library reading but she's actually quite a go-getter, action fighter. She'll take you by surprise."

According to her grandmother Maureen, Jenna-Louise was named after Priscilla Presley's character in *Dallas* [*Jenna Wade*], and Maureen added:

Jenna is going to be great in Doctor Who. Acting is all she ever wanted to do. She started singing and dancing aged two and did little routines in the front room for us.

Mind you, she was scared of ghosts and monsters as a little girl.

Right at the start of the book, I revealed that I had acquired a signed photo from one of either Alex Kingston or Jenna-Louise Coleman—well, the book's last companion picture is fittingly that of Ms Coleman.

So how did my (desperate) search actually fare?

Well, from my list of twenty-six companions, the trace involved twenty-four—as Jacqueline Hill and Adrienne Hill had passed away long before I

Jenna-Louise Coleman

started the original book.

In total, I found eighteen of the actresses and obtained a signed photograph from seventeen—Bonnie Langford being the odd one out. Seventeen out of twenty-four—that's somewhere in the region of seventy-one percent, and overall I've awarded myself a slightly presumptuous A- with the additional comment: "A pretty good effort."

That's just about all, but as a reward/punishment (delete as appropriate) for getting this far, I have decided to complete *Desperately Seeking Susan Foreman* by taking a closer look at "Hide," the last story to be transmitted whilst work on this book was still in progress.

This is a terrific story, and as a standalone drama, Matt Smith's era has offered little by way of comparison. The main reasons are probably as follows: a small cast, a largely restricted setting, and a relatively simple plot that isn't overly concerned with the conceptual threads in which many viewers (me included) seem to have become entangled.

"Hide" was actually the first writing contribution from Neil Cross—he also penned the far less impressive "The Rings of Akhaten," which was actually transmitted before "Hide"—but in this particular tale (set in November 1974), Cross did a pretty good job of creating rounded, believable characters. This is no mean feat in a forty-five minute window, but the writer may well agree that his words are magnificently enhanced by the performances of Dougray Scott and Jessica Raine, who played Alec Palmer and Emma Grayling—the pair at the center of the ghost-hunting.

Within the opening sixty seconds, it is clear there is a connection between the two. This connection is explored and allowed to grow alongside the main storyline; the apparition that had been seen and heard down the centuries within the house that Palmer had made a deliberate point of purchasing—much to Clara's astonishment. His personal "haunting" comes from wartime events: "Because I killed and I caused to have killed," and whilst Palmer's bravery, intelligence, and integrity are beyond question, he is seemingly incapable of expressing his emotions towards Emma Grayling. Emma's feelings are obvious, but she has words of warning for the Doctor's new companion: "Don't trust him. There's a sliver of ice in his heart."

Well one of them.

Matt Smith is on top form as this adventure—and his relationship with Clara—develops. Witness his reaction to spotting some of Palmer's equipment: "Oh! Oh look! Oh lovely, the ACR99821! Nice action on the toggle switch. I do love a toggle switch!"

"Actually I like the word 'toggle'. Nice noun... excellent verb!"

As for the "ghost," the dialogue reveals that its shape or form "never changes" in photographs, and it can only be detected in the presence of a powerful psychic—and that would be Emma.

The Doctor and Clara search the house, finding a "cold spot" in the music room. They then head for the TARDIS to travel both back and forward in time, in order that the Doctor can take pictures of the same location at various stages in the Earth's history. These brief trips cover the whole of the planet's life cycle, a concept that Clara finds very difficult to deal with. In one moment she hasn't been born, then she's been dead for one hundred billion years; her body is somewhere in the ground, yet the Doctor is talking to her.

"We are all ghosts to you.... What can we *possibly* be?" Clara wonders.

"The only mystery worth solving," comes the Time Lord's cryptic reply.

For the record, by the time you read this, the riddle of Clara's real identity will have been explained, but for now we're still in the confusing stage.

Anyway, the photographs prove that the ghost is actually a traveler named Hila Tukurian, who is trapped in a pocket universe and running from a creature whose shadowy image is only briefly seen.

As the resident psychic, Emma needs to open a bridge between the dimensions, and to boost her powers she must wear a headset fitted with a blue crystal from the planet Metebelis III. This is a direct reference to the crystal from the Jon Pertwee stories "The Green Death" and "Planet of the Spiders," and it's probably just as well that Emma wasn't fully aware of the last time the crystal was used to enhance psychic images via a human host, as the experience proved fatal for Professor Clegg in the latter of those vintage adventures.

Now would be the time to question the Doctor's pronunciation of the crystal's home planet. Back in the seventies, it was Metebēlis (i.e. with the equivalent of a long syllable in classic poetic scanning on the third vowel), but the twenty-first century version is Metebĕlis (the breve, or short syllable giving a pronunciation equivalent to "Metebellis" as opposed to "Metebeelis"). A minor point, but an important one that I feel better for having made.

Emma is understandably concerned about what is about to happen: "Will it hurt?"

"No," replies the Doctor. "No, well . . . yes. Probably . . . a bit. Well quite a lot. I don't know, it might be agony. To be perfectly honest, I'll be interested to find out."

I'm not entirely sure that would have helped, but very soon a "worm hole" appears, into which the Doctor disappears à la "Primeval." The rescue of Hila Tukurian is successful, but the Doctor doesn't make it back through the worm hole. Emma needs to gather her strength—affording Palmer the chance to reveal his feelings—for a second attempt at bringing back the Doctor. Meanwhile, Clara runs to the TARDIS.

An amusing little scene follows, as Clara comes face to face with herself—it is a voice visual interface and the TARDIS has selected an image of the person whom Clara holds in the highest esteem.

Fortunately for all concerned, the TARDIS suddenly acquires the ability to fly to its intended destination; the Doctor is rescued and that appears to be that.

Except that the mysterious, quite scary, and not particularly good-looking alien is unveiled as a creature simply pining for its mate, and the Doctor therefore makes one further trip to reunite the pair and ensure the smooth running of this particular course of true love.

Whilst this clearly mirrors the burgeoning relationship between the altogether better looking Alec and Emma, I'm really not sure about this particular twist, although I would expect opinion will be divided and others will consider the "monsters in love" scenario as something that actually added to the story.

The *Quatermass* influence is evident in this piece of work, as is the writer's obvious love of the original *Doctor Who*. Cross creates moments of revelation for all the main protagonists, and Matt Smith is able to shine with a script that allows moments of comedy mixed with a need to show bravery in the face of very real fear. This is the eleventh Doctor at his brilliant best, and credit must be given to a writer who seems to understand both the character and the actor as well as producing a story that gives Smith the perfect chance to showcase his talent.

In truth, there isn't a weak link amongst the cast's main quartet, and it was excellent to see a fine, established movie actor such as Dougray Scott (whom I last saw as Arthur Miller in *My Week with Marilyn*) alongside the wonderful Jessica Raine (fresh from delivering yet another baby in *Call the Midwife*). Great casting, great performances, great story.

And, I hope, the shape of things to come!

But, for now, I really hope you've enjoyed the third and final installment of my quest. I hereby declare my desperately seeking days to be well and truly over!

BIBLIOGRAPHY

The following websites were used for research purposes:

www.bbc.co.uk
www.doctorwhoreviews.co.uk
www.tardis.wikia.com
And these are the sources of the part replicated articles and quotes:
www.outpostskaro.com
www.youtube.com/watch?v=HgGEwrmiSAM
www.denofgeek.com/tv/19407
www.bbc.co.uk/doctorwho/classic/webcasts/shada/interviews/ward/page9.shtml
www.dailyrecord.co.uk/entertainment/celebrity-interviews/actress-jenna-louise-coleman

www.ingramcontent.com/pod-product-compliance
Lightning Source LLC
Chambersburg PA
CBHW072159160426
43197CB00012B/2446